DR JOHNSON BY MRS THRALE

I MRS THRALE

Dr Johnson
by Mrs Thrale

THE 'ANECDOTES' OF

MRS PIOZZI

IN THEIR ORIGINAL FORM

EDITED AND

WITH AN INTRODUCTION

BY RICHARD INGRAMS

CHATTO & WINDUS

THE HOGARTH PRESS

LONDON

Published in 1984 by
Chatto & Windus · The Hogarth Press
40 William IV Street
London WC2N 4DF

All rights reserved. No part of this publication may be
reproduced, stored in a retrieval system, or transmitted
in any form, or by any means, electronic, mechanical,
photocopying, recording or otherwise, without the prior
permission of the publisher.

The text of this edition is a selection from
*Thraliana: The Diary of Mrs Hester Lynch Thrale
(Later Mrs Piozzi) 1776-1809*
edited by Katherine C. Balderston, 1942
(2nd edn 1951)
and has been authorized by
the Oxford University Press

British Library Cataloguing in Publication Data

Thrale, Mrs.
Dr. Johnson by Mrs. Thrale.
1. Johnson, Samuel, *1709-1784*—Biography
2. Authors, English—18th century—Biography
I. Title II. Ingram's, Richard
828'.609 PR3533

ISBN 0 7011 2833 X

Introduction, editorial compilation and notes
copyright © Richard Ingrams 1984

Design and illustrative compilation
copyright © Chatto & Windus 1984

Set and printed in Great Britain by
Clark Constable
Edinburgh London Melbourne

CONTENTS

LIST OF ILLUSTRATIONS
page vii

INTRODUCTION
page ix

DR JOHNSON BY MRS THRALE
page 1

NOTES
page 129

LIST OF ILLUSTRATIONS

    I MRS THRALE *frontispiece*

   II STREATHAM PLACE *page* 2

  III DR JOHNSON IN HEBRIDEAN COSTUME *page* 13

  IV DAVID GARRICK *page* 29

   V THE SITTING ROOM AT BOLT COURT *page* 41

  VI HENRY THRALE *page* 63

 VII SIR JOSHUA REYNOLDS *page* 88

VIII JAMES BOSWELL *page* 90

  IX OLIVER GOLDSMITH *page* 93

   X THE SUMMER HOUSE AT STREATHAM *page* 109

  XI DR JOHNSON *page* 125

INTRODUCTION

It was Mrs Thrale's misfortune to be maligned in one of the classics of English literature. In his immortal *Life of Johnson*, James Boswell, motivated by jealousy of a rival biographer and a rival for Johnson's affection, poured scorn on her literary efforts, accusing her of inaccuracy and malice. Boswell, too, deliberately played down the importance of her friendship with Johnson, perhaps the only thing in his life that brought him true happiness. It was Mr Thrale, not Mrs, who, according to Boswell, had been the main attraction for Johnson at Streatham Park.

Boswell's lead has been followed with few exceptions ever since by commentators and scholars who in peppery footnotes and asides have faithfully repeated his charges. Poor Mrs Thrale has been treated with varying degrees of condescension by men, many of whom still cannot forgive her for, as they see it, abandoning their hero in his old age and absconding with a comic Italian singer.

One does not have to be a militant feminist to see in this distortion the seeds of a male conspiracy. From Boswell onwards, it has been traditional to picture Johnson as a man's man, happiest when holding forth to his club cronies or trekking round the Hebrides with Boswell. His domestic world, which in the latter half of his life centred on the Thrales, has been relegated to the background. As for Mrs Thrale, her undignified love affair in middle age and the fact that she preferred a young lover to an old friend has been considered proof in some quarters that Johnson's affection for her was misplaced.

Mrs Thrale was born Hester Salusbury at Bodvel in Carnarvonshire in 1741. Her family was an ancient Welsh one but her father John Salusbury was a charming and rakish figure whose affairs were always in a state of confusion. In 1748 he went out to Nova Scotia to seek his fortune leaving his wife and daughter, their only child, to the care of relatives in London and the country. Hester meanwhile was taught French, Italian, Spanish by her mother and her aunt, Lady Salusbury. At the age of seventeen she began to learn Latin and to write poetry, which she continued to do for the rest of her life. Her father died in 1762 and in October 1763 at St Anne's church in Soho she married a rich Old Etonian brewer, Henry Thrale. She was twenty-two. She always claimed that she never loved Thrale and married him only to please her mother. The marriage was founded on mutual respect, however. She wrote of her husband: 'With regard to his wife, though little tender of her person, he is very partial to her understanding.' They set up home at Streatham Park, a handsome country house with a hundred acres of land, and it was here in 1765 that she first met Johnson.

'She is the first woman in the world,' Johnson later told Boswell, 'could she but restrain that wicked tongue of hers. She would be the only woman in the world could she but command that little whirligig.' Mrs Thrale was full of vitality. She was charming, effusive – but impulsive: she said and wrote the first thing that came into her head, so making the kind of trouble for herself that a more prudent woman would have avoided.

In appearance she described herself thus: 'The height four feet eleven only, and the waist though not a taper one quite in proportion. The neck rather longish and remarkably white – so much so as to create suspicions of its being painted – This however is particular only because the woman is a brown one, with chesnut hair and eyebrows of the same colour strongly mark'd over a pair of large – but light grey eyes . . . *Expression* there is *none* I think; and the grace – which resembles that of *foreigners* – is more acquired than natural: for strength and not delicacy was the original characteristick of the figure. By keeping genteel company however, and looking much at paintings, learning to dance almost incessantly, and chosing foreign models, not English Misses as patterns of imitations; some grace has been acquired . . .'

It was her vitality, her 'wit', that attracted Johnson. She was always in high spirits. 'Now I have known my mistress sixteen years,' Johnson said, 'and never saw her out of humour yet, except once upon Chester Wall.' Johnson, by nature melancholy, hypochondriacal and prone to brood, was drawn to people, especially women, who were his exact opposite in temperament. To a man like him, a widower who had spent the best part of his life in comparative poverty, Mrs Thrale had other advantages. She was married to a rich and hospitable husband, she lived in a large country house with twelve bedrooms and a lake, and she had a number of small and, to Johnson who had no family, delightful daughters. Shortly after his first meeting with the Thrales, Johnson became absorbed into the family and was given his own room at Streatham Park and at the Thrales' town house in Southwark. He acted as a tutor to the children and a magnet who attracted many of the great men and women of the time to the Thrales' table – Goldsmith, Burke, Fanny Burney, Boswell, Reynolds. Thanks to him, Mrs Thrale became the leading literary hostess of the day.

At the same time he gradually formed a relationship with Hester Thrale closer than he could manage with anyone else. To a modern reader it has to be stressed that there was no sexual element in it. Johnson was thirty-five years older than she was and, in her eyes, physically repulsive. She writes that his appearance was so strange that fear was the emotion he evoked at first sight; and until she met her second husband at the age of forty, Mrs Thrale was not really interested in what she called the 'tender passion'. Besides, like Johnson, she was a devout Christian who tried, not always successfully, to do her duty as a wife and mother. Their friendship was, however, very intimate, especially on Johnson's part. In her company he became relaxed and flirtatious. His letters to her, especially those he wrote from the Hebrides, are quite unlike anything else of his in their spirit of gaiety and good humour. When published in 1788 they forced Horace Walpole completely to revise his view of Johnson and cast Boswell, who now realised for the first time that Johnson had been far more intimate with her than with him – what's more, that he hardly ever mentioned him when writing to her – into a fit of such depression that he was unable to work for several days.

But there were times when Mrs Thrale found even her resources of vitality taxed. Johnson, an insomniac, often forced her to stay up half the night making tea and conversation. He confided in her all his secret and morbid thoughts, in particular his fear of insanity. He even persuaded her at one stage to lock him up in his room and beat him to cure him of what he thought was madness. 'Yet it is a very gloomy reflexion,' she wrote to him, 'that so much of bad prevails in our best enjoyments, and embitters the purest friendship.'

It was Johnson who persuaded Mrs Thrale to keep a commonplace book. It began life as an 'ana' – a collection of anecdotes – but later developed as more of a diary. Into it she poured her thoughts and into it she copied out verses by herself and others and recorded stories that she had heard at her dinner-table. She wrote, as she talked, in a gush without much care for punctuation and without worrying about whether she was repeating herself or not. Everything went in: her religious speculations; her rhapsodies over Piozzi; her observations of nature. By the time of her death in 1821 she had amassed a huge quantity of material, over 1,000 pages in all, enough to fill two large volumes which were eventually published in 1942.

Buried in these fat tomes is the material that she later re-shaped into her *Anecdotes of Dr Johnson* and which is now published separately for the first time in its original form.

The circumstances in which the *Anecdotes* were published were not favourable from the author's point of view. In 1781 Henry Thrale died after four distressing years of intermittent illness and depression. Mrs Thrale, who had never been warmly attached to her husband, promptly fell in love for the first time in her life, with an Italian musician Gabriel Piozzi, a singer and composer described by Anna Seward as 'a handsome man with gentle pleasing and unaffected manners, and with very eminent skill in his profession'. The general opinion, however, was that Piozzi was unsuitable; he was foreign, he was a Catholic and he was her social inferior. Some people, including Boswell, hoped that Mrs Thrale would marry Johnson, thereby showing how little they knew her. Johnson himself, now seventy-two and already in bad health, was probably wise enough to rule out such a remote possibility. But he no doubt hoped in his old age to continue to enjoy the friendship of Mrs Thrale, the comforts of Streatham and the ministrations of his hostess. Unable to confide in Johnson and knowing that like all her friends and family he disapproved of Piozzi, Mrs Thrale spent two or three years in a state of dither, confusion and sometimes hysteria. In October 1782, partly to help sever the link with Johnson, she let her Streatham house and retired to Bath. To appease her daughters she renounced Piozzi; then, when she went into a further nervous decline, the daughters relented and Piozzi was recalled. At last on July 23rd, 1784 they were married and sailed for a long honeymoon on the Continent. Three months later Johnson died. He had tried to remain indifferent and suppress his feelings but his anger, jealousy and self-pity from time to time gained the upper hand and he railed against Piozzi or burned some of Mrs Thrale's letters. It was an ironic ending to the life of a man who had always set his face against 'canting' and who, had any other woman been involved, would have dismissed the public hysteria over Mrs Thrale's marriage to a foreigner and a Roman Catholic as the purest variety of humbug.

Johnson's death led to a frenzy of activity on the biographical front. Writers retired to their desks and, seizing their pens, strove to be first into print with their memoirs of the great man. Despite the pleasures of marriage and travel, Mrs Thrale was unable to resist the challenge. She had her commonplace books with her in Italy, though her many letters from Johnson were locked up in a safe in London. She was soon able to dispatch a manuscript to her publishers and the book came out, ahead of the field, on March 25th, 1786. The first edition of 1,000 copies sold out in a day, even King George III finding it hard to come by a copy.

Mrs Thrale would have done better to have taken her time. But she had a number of personal motives for rushing into print. Her reputation in England, which as a famous hostess she greatly valued, was at its lowest following her marriage. A successful book would help to restore her to public favour as well as laying the foundation for a career as a literary lady. Added to which, no doubt, she felt guilty about her neglect of Johnson during his final years. Now she would have an opportunity to show something of his other side; his rudeness, his melancholy, all the things that had made her dread the prospect of looking after him on his deathbed.

As a result of the speed with which she compiled her book and the secondary motives she had for writing it, she left out much of the best material in the original. Some of the anecdotes did not fit conveniently into her sequence. Many of Johnson's more outspoken remarks she perhaps thought unsuitable, for example his comment on Dr Burney's music book – 'The words are well arranged – but I don't understand one of them'; or his uncharitable opinion of Miss Harriet Poole – 'How pleasing would this girl's softness and innocency be if she had anything else besides softness and innocency!' She included that part of a conversation in which she compared Johnson to an elephant but omitted his previous comparison of her to a rattlesnake – 'for many have felt your venom, few have escaped your attractions, and all the world knows you have the rattle'. (That was something her enemies, especially Boswell, would no doubt have seized on!)

Others of Johnson's opinions were left out in the published version, perhaps because Mrs Thrale in her hurry to get her book out before her rivals simply overlooked them. There are a number of typically Johnsonian *mots* which were not included:

> 'Modern poetry is like modern gardening, everything now is raised by a hot bed; everything therefore is forced, and everything tasteless.'
> 'I never yet saw a Frenchman's gaiety as good as an Englishman's drunkenness.'
> 'An officer is seldom *bright* indeed, but he is almost always *smooth*.'

Sometimes Mrs Thrale in her zeal to refurbish her material for publication robbed it of its force. Instead of trusting her original record she padded it out, translating Johnson's simple monosyllabic words – many of which she had written down almost on the spot – into Johnsonese, the sort of portentous prose which readers who knew him only from his books would expect to emerge from his lips.

Here are two brief examples of her rewording:

'This dog would have been a fit member of the society established by Lycurgus, she condemns one to a state of perpetual vigilance.' (*Thraliana*)

'This animal would have been of extraordinary merit and value in the state of Lycurgus: for she condemns one to the exertion of perpetual vigilance.' (*Anecdotes*)

'When a person is hurrying to the grave upon full speed – a physician may give them a turn; – yet if they keep on a regular and slow pace, no care can save them.' (*Thraliana*)

'When Death's pale horse runs away with persons on full speed, an active physician may possibly give them a turn; but if he carries them on an even slow pace, down hill too! no care nor skill can save them!' (*Anecdotes*)

According to Katherine C. Balderston, editor of *Thraliana* (1942), five-ninths of the published *Anecdotes* consist of passages taken from the diaries. She adds, 'The remaining four-ninths is partly composed of introductions, flourishes and general lucubrations, and partly of course of actual new matter which was, of course, either recalled from memory, or invented, and is therefore less reliable than the passages borrowed from the *Thraliana*.'

These *Thraliana* passages are now printed separately for the first time. The bulk of the material comprises one long continuous passage of about 20,000 words. This was written by Mrs Thrale between September and December 1777 and some of it was copied from an earlier note-book called *Johnsoniana*, only fragments of which survive. The remainder of this book consists of shorter passages extracted from the diary and printed in sequence. These come to a virtual halt at the time of the break with Johnson in 1783, though Mrs Thrale continued until her death in 1821 to cherish his memory and was always accompanied on her travels by his portrait and a collection of his books.

The text has been copied from the 1942 edition of *Thraliana* with only minimal changes. Mrs Thrale's punctuation, or rather lack of it, has been faithfully preserved, though I have broken up her lengthy passages with sideheadings and paragraphing of my own. Many of Mrs Thrale's own footnotes are included and other notes added by me are given at the end of the book.

RICHARD INGRAMS, ALDWORTH 1984

Publisher's Note

The original footnotes by Mrs Thrale
are marked in the text thus, †.
Richard Ingrams' notes are flagged in the text *,
and can be found
at the end of this volume
under the relevant page number.

DR JOHNSON BY MRS THRALE

II STREATHAM PLACE

Preface ∽ In order to accomplish that purpose, and to delight myself by committing to Paper the regard I have for Mr Johnson, I shall begin this Book by mentioning such little Anecdotes concerning his Life, his Character, and his Conversation, as I have been able to collect: All my Friends reproach me with neglecting to write down such Things as drop from him almost perpetually, and often say how much I shall some Time regret that I have not done't with diligence ever since the commencement of our Acquaintance: They say well, but ever since that Time I have been the Mother of Children, and little do these wise Men know or feel, that the Crying of a young Child, or the Perverseness of an elder, or the Danger however trifling of any one – will soon drive out of a female Parent's head a Conversation concerning Wit, Science or Sentiment, however She may appear to be impressed with it at the moment: besides that to a *Mere de famille* doing something is more necessary & suitable than even hearing something; and if one is to listen all Even^g and write all Morning what one has heard; where will be the Time for tutoring, caressing, or what is still more useful, for having one's Children about one: I therefore charge all my Neglect to my young ones Account, and feel myself at this moment very miserable that I have at last, after being married fourteen Years and bringing eleven Children,* leisure to write a *Thraliana* forsooth; – though the second Volume *does* begin with Mr Johnson.

Our First Meeting ∽ It was on the second Thursday of the Month of January 1765. that I first saw Mr Johnson in a

Room: Murphy* whose Intimacy with Mr Thrale had been of many Years standing, was one day dining with us at our house in Southwark; and was zealous that we should be acquainted with Johnson, of whose Moral and Literary Character he spoke in the most exalted Terms; and so whetted our desire of seeing him soon, that we were only disputing *how* he should be invited, *when* he should be invited, and what should be the pretence. at last it was resolved that one Woodhouse a Shoemaker who had written some Verses, and been asked to some Tables, should likewise be asked to ours, and made a Temptation to Mr Johnson to meet him: accordingly he came, and Mr Murphy at four o'clock brought Mr Johnson to dinner – We liked each other so well that the next Thursday was appointed for the same Company to meet – exclusive of the Shoemaker, and since then Johnson has remained till this Day, our constant Acquaintance, Visitor, Companion and Friend.

Johnson's Parents ∽ Mr Johnson was a Man of mean Birth; his Father a Bookseller at Lichfield, his Mother's Extraction was higher, her Maiden Name was Ford, and the Parson* who sits next the Punch Bowl in Hogarth's modern Midnight Conversation was her Brother's Son.

His Father was a pious and a worthy Man he says, but wrong-headed, positive, and afflicted with Melancholy; which his Son observed once to me would have been more perceptible, had not the perpetual Pressure of his pecuniary Affairs kept him waking to one particular Thing. his Business likewise led him to be much on Horseback, which probably contributed not a little to his Health & Spirits: he was still a larger & stouter bodied Man than Mr Johnson who was thought very like him; he was 56. when he married his Wife who was herself 41. and they had two Sons at the Distance of three Years between. The Father died of an Inflammatory

Feaver at the Age of 76 – the Mother of a gradual Decay at the Age of 89. She was however slight in her Person, & rather below than above the middle Size. So excellent was her Character and so blameless her Life, that when an oppressive Neighbour once endeavoured to rob her of a little Field She had, he could perswade no Attorney to undertake his Cause against a Woman so much beloved by her little Circle. I suppose every body knows as well as I do, that it is her Character which he has drawn in the Poem upon the Vanity of human Wishes

  The general fav'rite as the general Friend &c &c –

The Queen's Evil ∽ At two Years old his Mother brought him up to London to be touched by Queen Anne, for the Evil which greatly afflicted him in his Childhood, & left such Marks as even now greatly disfigure his Countenance, besides the irreparable damage it has done to the Auricular Organs; & I suppose 'tis owing to that horrible Disorder too that he never could make use but of one Eye, this defect however was never visible, both Eyes look exactly alike. I have asked him whether he remembered Queen Anne at all; he thought he had some confused Remembrance of a Lady in a black Hood.

His Old Maid Catharine ∽ His Mother and her old Maid Catharine taught him to read, and he recollected very perfectly sitting in Katharine's Lap, and reading the Story of Saint George & the Dragon: I know not whether this is the proper Place to add that such was his Tenderness, and such his Gratitude that he took a Journey to Lichfield 55 Years afterwards to support & comfort [her], in her last Illness. he had enquired for his Nurse, but She was dead.*

He likewise remembered the first time his Mother ever told him about heaven & Hell, he was in Bed with her he said, & to impress it still stronger on his Memory She bid him tell Thomas Jackson a favourite Workman – when he arose what She had said to him.

Scruples of Infidelity ↝ At eight Years old he went to School, for his Health would not permit him to go sooner, & at the Age of Ten Years his Mind was disturbed by Scruples of Infidelity, which preyed upon his Spirits and made him very uneasy: the more so perhaps as he revealed his Uneasiness to no one being naturally of a sullen Temper & reserved Disposition: he however searched diligently but fruitlessly for Evidences of the Christian Faith, till at length recollecting a Book he had once picked up in the Shop, & again thrown by, entitled *De Veritate Relig*:* &c. he began to think himself highly culpable for neglecting such a means of Information and took himself severely to task for this Sin. The first Opportunity he had of Course he examined the Book with avidity, but finding his Scholarship insufficient for the perusal of it he set his heart at rest it seems, and considered his Conscience as lightened of a Crime: he thought however from the pain which Guilt had given him, that the Soul's Immortality could no longer be disputed, & resolving from that Time to become a Christian, he became one of the most zealous and pious ones ever known.

When he had told me this particular Anecdote of his Childhood one Evening; I cannot imagine says he on a sudden what makes me talk of myself to you so, unless it is that Confidence begets Confidence, for I never did relate this foolish Story to any one but to Dr Taylor* & my Wife, not even to my poor dear Bathurst,* whom I loved above all living Creatures.

Hamlet ↝ He once told me another Accident of his younger Years, which however I have no Reason to think I have to myself: he was just nine Years old when having got the play of Hamlet to read in his Father's Kitchen, he read on very qu[i]etly till he came to the Ghost Scene, when he hurried up Stairs to the Shop Door that he might see folks about him. This Story he was not unwilling to tell as a Testimony to the Merits of Shakespear.

Characters of the Rambler ∽ Let me now tell one for a Testimony to his own as a Writer. When the Rambler* first came out in Numbers it was universally read; and at Rumford in Essex the People were particularly fond of it, till observing how natural many of the Characters were, they began to fit them to each other & suspect that Cupidus was meant to represent one of the Inhabitants – Captator another & so on till they were perfectly well perswaded that one of the Members of their Bowling Green Club, wrote these Papers to amuse himself at the Expence of the rest. To detect the false Brother, and expose his Treachery – they wrote to Collins a Bookseller at Salisbury enquiring who was the Authour of the Rambler, Mr Collins replied it was one Samuel Johnson, a Writer who seemed likely to succeed in the World. Most unfortunately this was the name of their Minister, whom they reprimanded severely; and observed that all the Morality of his Papers should not atone for his ridiculing his Friends in so cruel a manner – the character of Leviculus is mine I hear added the Accuser – but I will have *some* Satisfaction. The Clergyman who found all Protestations vain, was forced to go to London & find the Authour, who had never seen Rumford in his Life: – & who by readily owning the Incendiary Papers – gave Peace to the Bowling Green Club.

His Ramblers however are very often Portraits: That of Prospero is I suppose well known to be Garrick's that of Sophron a Country Gentleman whose name he has now forgot – that of Gelidus one Coulson a Mathematician who lived at Rochester: the Man mentioned [in] N⁰ 4 for purring like a Cat was one Busby I believe a Proctor in the Commons, & he who barked so ingeniously, and then called the Drawer to drive away the Dog, was Father to Dʳ Salter of the Charter house; he who Sung a Song and by correspondent motions of his hand chalked a Gyant on the Wall was one Richardson an Attorney – and I suppose no one needs Information that by Cantilenus was meant Dʳ Percy. The Character of Sober in the Idler* however was his own, and he told me he had his own Outset into Life in his Eye when he wrote the Eastern Story of Gelaleddin – by Bassora was meant Oxford of Course.

The Letter signed Sunday was it seems written by Miss Talbot. Mʳˢ Eliz: Carter wrote the Allegory of Religion & Superstition, and the Letter sign'd Chariessa; – The Billets in the 1ˢᵗ Vol: were sent him by Mʳˢ Chapone, then known by the Name of Miss Mulso.

Feigned Names ↩ Baretti* and I once tried to write out a List of all the Things he had written in feigned Names, many of which he has himself I doubt not forgotten by now, besides Prefaces, Dedications Introductions &c. out of Number, done for People in Distress who wanted Money Wit or advice from him – Murphy says, that charging him the other Day with writing Dodd's Sermon* & Kelly's Prologue* – why Sir says he when they come to me with a dead Staymaker and a dying Parson – What can a Man do?

Johnson's Verses ↩ One Day in the Year 1768 I saw some Verses with his Name in a Magazine these are they –

VERSES,
Said to have been written by Samuel
Johnson, L. L. D. *at the request of a Gentleman
to whom a Lady had given a Sprig of Myrtle.*

[8]

> WHAT hopes, what terrors does thy gift create,
> Ambiguous emblem of uncertain fate!
> The Myrtle (ensign of supreme command
> Consign'd by Venus to Melissa's hand)
> Not less capricious then a reigning fair,
> Oft favours, oft rejects a lover's pray'r:
> In Myrtle shades oft sings the happy swain.
> In Myrtle shades despairing ghosts complain;
> The Myrtle crowns the happy lover's heads,
> Th' unhappy lovers graves the Myrtle spreads;
> O! then the meaning of thy gift impart,
> And ease the throbbings of an anxious heart,
> Soon must this bough, as you shall fix his doom,
> Adorn Philander's head, or grace his tomb.

I thought they were not his so I asked him; – A young fellow† replied he about forty Years ago, had a Sprig of Myrtle given him by a Girl he courted, and asked me to write him some Verses upon it – I promised but forgot; & when the Lad came a Week after for them, I said I'll go fetch them so ran away for five Minutes, & wrote the nonsense you are so troubled about; & which these Blockheads are printing now so pompously with their L.L:D.

This Facility of writing, and this dilatoriness to write, Mr Johnson always retained; & I think the finest Paper he ever wrote was that upon the Subject of Procrastination which he begun and ended in Sir Joshua Reynolds's parlour while the Man waited to carry it to press.

Advice to Young People ⁓ Mr Johnson had by his own account never been a close Student & us'd to advise young People never to be without a little Book in their Pocket to read at by Times when they had nothing else to do. it has been by that means chiefly added he, that all my Knowlege has been gained, except what I have picked up by running about the

† Edmund Hector of Birmingham.

World with my Wits ready to observe & my Tongue willing to talk: a Man is seldom in a humor to unlock his Book Case; set out his Desk and betake him seriously to study, but a retentive Memory will do something, and a fellow shall have strange Credit given him, if he can but recollect striking Passages from a few Books, keep the Authors separate in his Head, & bring his Stock of Knowledge artfully into Play.

His Dictionary however could not one would think have been done by running up & down, but he really never did consider it himself as a great Performance, and used to say he might have done it with Ease in two Years Time had he been blessed with Diligence & Health. Baretti used to say very properly "had I had Johnson's Genius, or he had my Spirit of Application & Drudgery; we might have driven our Coaches and Six long ago."

I have however often thought that Mr Johnson was more free than prudent, in telling so carelessly that he was not a very complete Scholar, in Greek particularly, for few would have believed it had he not proclaimed it so, and Doctor Parker's insulting him one Day at Brighthelmston obliged him to retort the Imputation of Ignorance in such a Manner as distressed every one present.

Reputation ∽ I know it is his Principle to treat Reputation slightly; for speaking one day on this Subject, he said: A Man Sir must depend on the main Trunk of his Character, conscious that Leaves will fall with ev'ry Wind, & even a tolerable Twig sometimes, if touched with a hasty Finger.

Pope ∽ On something a similar Subject, when Tom Davies* printed the fugitive Pieces without his Knowledge or Consent; what says I would Pope have done had they served him so? we should never have heard the last on't to be sure replied he but then Pope Madam was a narrow Man.

Of Pope as a Writer he had however the highest Opinion. Talking of his own Preface to Shakespear, of which I had then seen only the proof Sheet; as superior to Pope's: I fear not says he, the little Fellow has done Wonders.

Payment ∽ Johnson was always unwilling to touch Pen & Ink without being paid for it; would I believe make rather a hard Bargain, than an easy one & once observed to Mr Thrale that A Man never gave that away freely he was used to sell, or delighted in doing that Gratis which he was wont to be paid for: would you not rather added he make any Man a present of Money than of Porter?

Faults in the Dictionary ∽ In pursuance of this Principle I remember we had one Day – seven Years ago I suppose or ten perhaps; put him in Mind of four or five faults in his Dictionary, & express'd our Wishes for a new Edition: Alas Sir said he there are four or five hundred Faults instead of four, but it would take me up three Months Labour, & when the Time was out, the Work would not be done. The Booksellers set him about it soon after however, & he went chearfully enough to his Business – *moyennant les Ecus* as the French say.

The Frogs ∽ It was comical when somebody complimented him upon his Dictionary & mentioned the Ill Success of the French in a similar Attempt. Why what would you expect says he of Fellows that eat Frogs.

He was indeed willing enough at all Times to express his hatred & Contempt of our Rival Nation, & one day when a Person mentioned them as agreeable from their Gaiety – I never yet says Johnson saw a Frenchmans Gaiety as good as an Englishman's Drunkenness.

Johnson at Versailles ↷ When we were together seeing the Theatre at Versailles,* we went on the Stage to examine the Machinery – & now said I What shall we act? The Englishman in Paris? No replies Johnson, let us act *Harry the fifth*.

French Style ↷ Baretti & he were talking one Day of foreign Literature; Mr Baretti praising his Countrymen & depreciating the French; Give them however said he the praise of Style at least; French Literature resembles French Dinners I believe; they have few Sentiments but they express them elegantly, they have little Meat too but they dress it well.

French Diet ↷ He changed his opinion indeed with regard to the Eatables, after his Journey to the Continent; Every man said he there, feeds from the Earth nearly – that's immediately, or remotely, the Englishman eats the Ox which eat the Grass; The Frenchman eats the Grass himself I see, and leaves none for the Cattle.

Corneille & Shakespeare ↷ When he was serious he was however not unwilling to pay his Tribute of Respect to their Philosophers, Scholars & Wits; when talked to one day concerning a Comparison to be drawn between Shakespeare & Corneille he said – Corneille is to Shakespeare as a clipped Hedge to a Forest.

The Scotch ↷ We all know how well he loved to abuse the Scotch, & indeed to be abused by them in return. To one of them who commended the Town of Glasgow he replied – Sir I presume you have never yet seen Brentford, Mr Boswell said the Man read Lectures against him afterwards by way of revenge, and to be told so seem[ed] to flatter him. He loved Mr Boswell sincerely, & well he might: for

III DR JOHNSON IN HEBRIDEAN COSTUME

>Scarce to Heav'n one could excuse
>The Devotion he did use
>Unto that adored Name.†

Johnson & Boswell put me in Mind of Cato & Juba; I told them so, & both were pleased: Miss Reynolds said, Johnson & Beauclerc put her in mind of Socrates & Alcibiades, & both of them were pleased.

Lord Bute ∽ The Story of Johnson's saying how Literature in Scotland was distributed like Bread in a besieged Town; to every Man a Mouthful, & to no Man a Bellyful; is so well known it is not worth recording: Lord Bute it seems when he heard it first said – Well! Well! the Fellow must have a Pension however – this he told me himself.

God Made Hell ∽ When Mr Johnson returned from his Journey to the North in the year 1773. Strahan the King's Printer accosted him with Well Sir! and what think you of my Country now? That it is a very poor Country surely said Mr Johnson: Well well! God made it Sir cries Strahan displeased; "'true enough Sir he did so, but he made it for Scotsmen – and Comparisons are odious Mr Strahan, but God made Hell!'"

No Trees ∽ The Scotch I think never forgave his saying they had no Trees in their Country & one of them once mentioning a beautiful Prospect to be seen there; Johnson instantly observed that he had omitted the most beautiful they possessed; which was the Prospect of the Road from Edinburgh to London.

His Repartie ∽ Every body I suppose remembers his famous Repartie to Dr Blair who to prove the Authenticity of

† of Johnson.

[14]

Ossians Poems* asked him if any Man living could write such; Yes surely Sir replies Mr Johnson – many Men, many Women, & many Children.

Mr Pottinger ∽ He was one Day likewise very happy in a Retort upon Pottinger who had pecked at him so long that Fitzmaurice, whose house they dined at began to fret, & observed that Mr Pottinger opposed him so petulantly for no better Reason than that he might the next Day tell his Friends at the Club how he had had the Honor of disputing with Johnson – *Honour* says Pottinger hastily – I see no honour in it: Well Sir replies Mr Johnson – if you don't see the *Honour*, I feel the *Disgrace*.

A Coxcomb ∽ Ah Sir says a Coxcomb one Day at our Table while Pepys* and Johnson were talking about Literature – I have lost all my Greek – Ay Sir replies Johnson and I on the same day lost all my Estate in Yorkshire.

Lord Bolingbroke ∽ The Story of his calling Ld Bolingbroke* a Coward because he charged his Gun to let fly in the Face of Christianity, & then paid a hungry Scotsman for drawing the Trigger after his Death has been I suppose in every Mouth & in every Jest Book, but one has now & then a coarse Joke of his partly to one's self; For example poor Miss Owen said meekly enough one Day ""I am sure my Aunt was exceedingly sorry when the Report was raised of Mr Thrale's death"" – Not sorrier I suppose replied Mr Johnson than the Horse is when the Cow miscarries.

Too Much Praise ∽ If in short any one, or even himself had bestowed more Praise on a Person or Thing than he thought they deserved he would instantly rough them and that in a Manner brutal enough to be sure; at Sir Robert Cotton's

Table I once inadvertently commended the Pease – which I have since thought were too little boyl'd – adding, – taste these Pease Mr Johnson do, are not they charming? – Yes Madam replied he – For a Pig.

Sir Joshua ∾ It was at Streatham however, & before Murphy Baretti, Lyttelton & multis aliis, that he served Sir Joshua Reynolds saucily enough: the Conversation turned upon Painting – I am sorry says our Doctor to see so much Mind laid out on such perishable Materials – Canvass is so slight a Substance, and your Art deserves to be recorded on more durable Stuff, why do you not paint oftener upon Copper? Sir Joshua urged the Difficulty of getting a Plate large enough for Historical Subjects & was going on to raise further Objections, when Mr Johnson fretting that he had so inflamed his friend's Vanity I suppose, – suddenly and in a surly Tone replied What's here to do with such Foppery? has not Thrale here got a thousand Tun of Copper? you may paint it all round if you will, it will be no worse for him to brew in – afterwards.

Making Amends ∾ On the other Hand if he had unawares spoken harshly to a modest man, he would strive to make him amends as in the following Case. A young Fellow of great Fortune as he was sitting with a Book in his hand at our House one Day called to him rather abruptly – & he fancied disrespectfully – Mr Johnson says the Man – would you advise me to marry? I would advise *no Man* to marry answered he, bouncing from his Chair & leaving the Room in a fret – that is not likely to propagate Understanding. The young Fellow looked confounded & had barely begun to recover his Spirits when the Doctor returned with a smiling Countenance and joining in the General Prattle of the Party, turned it insensibly to the Subject of Marriage;

where he laid himself out in a Conversation so entertaining instructive & gay that nobody remembered the Offence except to rejoyce in its Consequences.

A Compliment ~ Nothing indeed seem[s] to flatter him more than to observe a Person struck with his Conversation whom he did not expect to be so; & this happened to him particularly in Company with the famous Daniel Sutton who at that time inoculated one of my Children and who was a Fellow of very quick Parts I think, though as ignorant as dirt both with regard to Books and the World. The following Thoughts I remember made the Man stare as we call it, and seemed to throw a new Light upon his Mind. – Money chanced to be the Topick of the Morning Talk, and Mr Johnson observed that it resembled Poyson, as a small Quantity would often produce fatal Effects; but given in large Doses though it might sometimes prove destructive to a Weak Constitution, yet it might often be found to work itself off, & leave the Patient well. He took notice in the Course of the same Conversation that all Expence was a kind of Game, wherein the Skilful player catches and keeps what the unskilful suffers to slip out of his Hands. Sutton listened and grinned and gaped & said at last – half out of Breath I never kept such Company before and cannot tell how to set about leaving it now. – the Compliment though awkward pleased our Doctor much, & no wonder; it was likely to please both Vanity & Virtue.

Johnson's Little Strokes ~ Johnson as he was just in every Thing, was scrupulously so in giving Characters of living People, but he had not great Opportunities of knowing them; few would expose their Passions or their Oddities before so universal a Censor, and his want of Sight or hearing often made him liable to lose such *Traits* as would have changed his Opinions had they come within his reach: little Strokes however he would sometimes give that like the Sketches of Raphael are worth more than the finish'd Pictures of inferior Hands, I will write out a few that I remember.

Murphy ☙ Of Murphy when I extolled his Talents for Conversation – tis certain says Mr Johnson that that Man by some happy Skill displays more knowledge than he really has; like Gamesters who can play for more Money than they are worth: he has however so due a Mixture of Invention & of Narrative, of Fact & Sentiment that few are so likely to please.

Lady Cotton ☙ Of Lady Cotton* when I praised her Sweetness of Temper, he reply'd tis true, but one no more thanks her for being sweet than one thanks a Honeycomb; it is her Nature and She cannot help it.

Catherine Wynne ☙ Of Lady Catherine Wynne he said that She was like sour Small beer; She could not says he have been a good Thing; & even that bad thing was spoil'd.

Peter King ☙ Of Peter King* when I asked his Opinion he replied; It is a Mind in which nothing has grown up of itself & where whatever has been transplanted – has degenerated.

Lady Macdonald ☙ For Lady Macdonald* he had a worse Denunciation – That Woman says He is no other than a dead Nettle, were She alive She would sting.

Dr Lawrence's Daughter ☙ Of Doctor Lawrence's* Daughter he said one Day, that Girl knows Greek surprizingly but She knows nothing else; and surely an empty Pate adorned with Literature will do but little for the Wench: Tis like setting Diamonds in Lead methinks, it can only obscure the Lustre of the Stone, and make the Possessor ashamed on 't.

Harriott Poole ↫ Of Miss Harriott Poole* says he, how pleasing would this Girl's Softness and Innocency be if She had any thing else besides Softness & Innocency! but She is nothing, and can be nothing, and so one thanks her for nothing I think.

Mrs Thrale ↫ For my own Part he told me once that of all Animals he had found out that which I most resembled, it is says He – The Rattle Snake; for many have felt your Venom, few have escap'd your Attractions, and all the World knows you have the Rattle.

In return I observed to him that he most resembled an Elephant: whose Weight could crush the Crocodile, & whose Proboscis could from its Force and Ductility either lift up the Buffalo, or pick up the Pin.

Ralph Plumbe ↫ Of Ralph Plumbe* at the Time he was dying –: he said – I feel that I should be more concern'd for the Dog – the Dog is commonly equal to his Character, and the Lad is below his.

When we talked of introducing that same Fellow into Company – He will learn nothing in any Company quoth Johnson; such people are like Cork'd Bottles you may put them into Water, if you will, & under Water, but they get no fuller.

A Whining Lady ↫ A whining Lady was lamenting her Misfortunes, when we thought no great harm had befallen her; I pity [her] says I however, She cries so; one cannot surely replies Mr Johnson pity *her* crying as much as the *Cat's*; but it would indeed be a cruel Disposition of Affairs, were we obliged to share Pain with those with whom we cannot share Pleasure.

A Creaking Door ↷ A Gentleman we knew was plagued with a complaining Wife who whimpered & teized the Man incessantly – 'tis sad for the poor Fellow to be tormented so said I; no Madam answers Johnson *he* does not hear her whimper; when A creaking door has creaked on for a fortnight, the Master will seldom give six Pence for having it oyl'd.

A Stupid Wife ↷ I observed a Man fond of a stupid Wife once; how can he be happy with such a Creature cry'd I? Madam Such Marriages replied the Doctor are like playing at Cards for nothing, no Passion is excited, and the Time is filled up.

Mrs Langton ↷ Of Mrs Langton* who was perpetually talking of the Players, he said; I once endeavoured to cure her; but perceiving I could put nothing in the Place of the exploded Subject, I felt myself in the Situation of a Physician who should prescribe light Food and light Wines to a dying Sailor in the South Seas, where nothing but salt Provisions were to be got.

Lead to a Feather ↷ When Cumberland* dedicated something to Romney* the Painter, I wonder says Mr Johnson what the Man thought he was doing now: it is nothing but tying Lead to a Feather; the Feather can never make the Lead swim, but the Lead will most certainly make the Feather sink.

Sir John Lade ↷ Lady Lade consulted him about her Son Sir John: endeavour Madam said he to procure him Knowlege; for really Ignorance to a rich man, is like Fat to a sick

Sheep, it only serves to call the Rooks about him. – on the same Occasion it was that he observed how a Mind unfurnished with Subjects and Materials for Thinking, can keep up no Dignity at all in Solitude – it is says he in the State of a Mill without Grist.

Fæculancies & Froth ∽ Mr Johnson had a great Notion of general Knowledge being necessary to a complete Character, and hated at his Heart a solitary Scholar who knew nothing but his Books. The Knowledge of Books says he will never do without looking on Life likewise with an observant Eye; much may indeed be swallowed, but much must be worked off; there are fæculancies which should subside, and Froth that shoud be scummed before the Wine can become fit for Drinking.

Nealy Ford's Advice ∽ Nealy Ford, his Relation the profligate Parson immortalized by Hogarth; was he told me the Man who advised him to study the Principles of every thing, that a general Acquaintance with Life might be the Consequence of his Enquiries – Learn said he the leading Precognita of all things – no need per[haps] to turn over leaf by leaf; but grasp the Trunk hard only, and you will shake all the Branches.

The Study of History ∽ Common, every Day Sense and a Power of Conversation on many Subjects was the Character Mr Johnson most delighted to meet with; for who but Swift says he, would think he was exalting a Female Character by telling how Vanessa could

      Name the ancient Heroes round – &c. &c.

and let nobody who reads this ill-compiled Nonsense now, suppose that he had such a respect for the Study of History, and the Lives of ancient Heroes that he meant to reserve such

Talk for *Men* by way of Preeminence – not he! he disliked the Subject exceedingly, & often said it took up room in a Man's head which might be better filled.

Education for Women ∽ With Regard to the female right to Literature 'tis plain by a Passage in M^r. Boswell's Journal that Johnson never disputed it: when his Friend consulted him whether he should give his Daughters a liberal Education or not – To be sure said he let them learn all they can learn – it is a paltry Trick indeed to deny Women the Cultivation of their mental Powers, and I think it is partly a proof we are afraid of them – if we endeavour to keep them unarmed.

Johnson Agrees with Rousseau ∽ Mr Johnson was however of Opinion that the Delicacy of the Sex shou'd always be inviolably preserved, in eating, in Exercise, in Dress, in every thing: & I often found his Ideas on this Topick in particular so conformable to those of Rousseau that sometimes it used to amaze me how very similar the two Minds must originally have been made; & how much both were altered from the first Resemblance by Education, Prejudices, Habits and Aims.

Steele's Essays ∽ It was on the 18: day of July 1773 that we were sitting in the blue Room at Streatham and were talking of Writers – Steele's Essays were mentioned – but they are too thin said Mr Johnson; being mere Observations on Life and Manners without a sufficiency of solid Learning acquired from Books, they have the flavour, like the light French Wines you so often hear commended; but having no Body, they cannot keep.

Verbose Language ∽ Speaking of Mason, Gray &c. he said

The Poems they write must I should suppose greatly delight the Authors; they seem to have attained that which themselves consider as the Summit of Excellence, and Man can do no more: yet surely such unmeaning & verbose Language if in the Morning it appears to be in bloom, must fade before Sunset like Cloe's Wreath.

Swift's Style ∽ Of Swift's Style which I praised as beautiful he observed; that it had only the Beauty of a Bubble, The Colour says he is gay, but the Substance slight.

Dryden ∽ We talked of Dryden – Buckingham's Play said I has hurt the Reputation of that Poet, great as he was; such is the force of Ridicule! – on the contrary my Dearest replies Doctor Johnson The greatness of Dryden's Character is even now the only principle of Vitality which preserves that Play from a State of Putrefaction.

Samuel Richardson ∽ To Richardson as a Writer he gave the highest Praises, but mentioning his unquenchable Thirst after Applause That Man said he could not be content to sail gently down the Stream of Fame, unless the Foam was continually dashing in his Face, that he might taste it at Every Stroke of the Oar.

Biographers ∽ We chatted on about Authors till we talked of him himself, when he frankly owned he had never worked willingly in his Life *Man or Boy* nor ever did fairly make an Effort to do his best except three Times whilst he was at School, nor that he ever made it his Custom to read any of his Writings before he sent it to Press – Well now said I that will not be believed, even if your Biographer should relate it, which too perhaps he will not: I wonder said he who will be my Biographer? Goldsmith to be sure I replied if you should go first – and he would do it better than any body. – but then he would do maliciously says Johnson – As for that answered I we should all fasten upon him & make him do Justice in spite of himself. but the worst is the Doctor does not know your Life, nor in Truth can I tell who does, unless it be Taylor of Ashbourne: why Taylor is certainly said he well enough acquainted with my History at Oxford, which I believe he has nearly to himself, but Doctor James can give a better Account of my early Days than most Folks, except Mr Hector of Birmingham & little Doctor Adams. After my coming to London you will be at a Loss again; though Jack Hawkesworth and Baretti both, with whom I lived quite familiarly, can tell pretty nearly all my Adventures from the Year 1753. however I intend to disappoint the Dogs, and either outlive them all or write my Life myself. But for a Johnsoniana cried I we will defy you at least; Boswell & Baretti; & myself from Time to Time have a trick of writing down Anecdotes Bons mots &c. & Doctor Percy will be busy at this work I warrant him: He would replied Mr Johnson, but I have purposely suffered him to be misled, and he has accordingly gleaned up many Things that are not true.

This Conversation passed on the 18: of July 1773 & I wrote it down that night, as I thought it particularly interesting: I have copied it out this 26: Novr 1777. and am shocked to find three of the People named in it all dead – Goldsmith Hawkesworth & Doctor James.

Dr James Beattie ⁓ Says Goldsmith to Reynolds at our Table one Day – they talk of Beattie for an Author; and what has Beattie done compared to me; who have written so many Volumes? Ah Doctor cries Johnson – who had listened till then – there go many Six pences to make one Guinea.

Young & Dryden ↪ We were speaking of Young as a Poet; Young's Works cried Johnson are like a miry Road, with here & there a Stepping Stone or so; but you must always so dirty your Feet before another clean Place appears, that nobody will often walk that way. In this however said I as well as in his general Manner of writing he resembles your favourite Dryden – & to this no Answer was made:

The next Morning we were drawing Spirits over a Lamp, and the Liquor bubbled in the Glass Retort;* there says Mr Johnson – Young bubbles & froths in his Descriptions like this Spirit; but Dryden foams like the Sea we saw in a Storm the other day at Brighthelmstone.

Brighthelmstone ↪ Of Brighthelmstone* itself he said This is a Country so truly desolate, that one's only Comfort is to think if one *had a* mind to hang Oneself, no Tree could be found on which to tye the Rope.

Mr Angelo ↪ I mentioned Mr Angelo – a Fencing Rascal says Johnson, – no really reply'd I, & though you don't love Fencing – many People do – So answered he I *love* Roast Beef, but yet I would not set the Turnspit to Table.

Sir Lucas Pepys ↪ Pepys came in Turn to be talked of – He said I cannot love the Man: why says I to be sure the Master does talk pompously of some Things that you despise, as Gardening for example – I have cried Mr Johnson no Objection to a Man rattling a Rattlebox – only don't let him think that he Thunders.

A Loss to the Turnpikes ↪ When the Duke of York died – though so greatly despised in his Life Time says somebody, he will now he is dead be a Loss – Very likely answers Johnson – to the Turnpikes.

Johnson's Sense of Humour ~ Mr Johnson's vein of humour was quite peculiar to himself, and few people seem to Think he possesses any; but Murphy whose Opinions on such a point cannot be controverted, has often agreed with me that there was real dry humour in his Disposition, and his Mirth had always something in it that forced others to be merry whenever he was disposed to Gayety.

I shewed him the other Day six small Ponies drawing a Four Wheel Chaise – what a Whim is this now said he to delight in mere Depravation! would it not be as pretty a Frolick to drive six spavined Horses all spavined of the same Leg.

Burke in a Bag ~ A Gentleman was talking at our Table of Mr Burke; and relating what a Philosopher he was, what a researcher into the works of Nature &c. Sir says the Man I saw him once go down into a Coal mine – in *a bag*: to see the People at work; he went in *a Bag* I say because of his Clothes; but he valued no Clothes, nor any thing else indeed when he was seeking for Knowledge, and I well remember that his Coat was spoyl'd – notwithstanding He went *in a Bag*. here the Gentleman paused, looking gravely at Johnson as if expecting a Reply – Well Sir! returns the Doctor; when we write his Life this Adventure shall be celebrated, and the Chapter which contains it shall be entitled – *Burke in a Bag*.

Francis Barber ~ The other Day speaking of his Negroe Francis;* I observed that he was very well-looking, for a Black a moor; Oh Madam says he Francis has carried the Empire of Cupid farther than many Men: When he was in Lincolnshire seven Years ago, he made hay as I was informed, with so much Dexterity that a female Hay Maker followed him to London for Love.

Poor Miss Owen ∽ When Miss Owen cry'd at the Thoughts of returning to Wales after a long Range among the Gay Folks of the Town – But think Madam says Johnson how your Conversation will illuminate the Montgomerians! – and besides there are some fine young Fellows grown up since your Departure from amongst them. He had before that made us all good Sport when we went together to Tunbridge & Brighthelmstone; saying how he would puff poor Miss Owen in the Rooms, & whisper People that *that* was the great Montgomeryshire Fortune; but when I find them fired says he with my Description, then I change my Voice, & Accent, & cry – but She is plaguy nice that I can tell you: – nice *indeed* Sir! – I offered her *myself* – but it would not do.

Burney's History of Music ∽ Burney* likewise has experienced his sportive Humour; when he shewed him his Book about Musick and enquired his Opinion concerning it; the Words are well arranged Sir replies Johnson – but I don't understand one of them.

Kit Smart ∽ Doctor Burney says he has a better Story of Johnson than any of us – concerning Kit Smart* who about a Dozen Years ago was confined for Lunacy. Says Burney I vex to hear of poor Kits going to Chelsey: – " "but a Madman must be confined Sir, – at Chelsey or elsewhere – " "Yes! but his general Health will probably suffer; such Restraint precludes all possibility of Exercise –" " Exercise replies Johnson! I never heard that he used any: he walked *to* the Ale house indeed, but then he was *carried* home again.

An Oxford Man ∽ I never say severe Things, you *know* I don't says Johnson but yesterday; no sure replied I, nor saucy ones neither; when I observed but last Sunday that there were five Cambridge Men in Company, & only you from Oxford – Yes but says You the Wolf don't count the Sheep – "'Well! come come, that was saucy enough; but a Man deserves to be an Oxford Man that talks *so*.'"

A Fellow in the Pillory ↬ A Fellow stood one Day in the Pillory as I passed by, the Mob was unruly, & like to demolish him: I could not get my head clear of the Wretch's Danger, & cry'd out once or twice perhaps in the Course of the Day – Poor Creature! how they pelted him! &c. at length Mr Johnson weary of the Subject said – Madam! think no more of him! He is drunk by now.

An Attorney ↬ It is reported of Mr Johnson & truly I believe; that sitting one Day in an Eating house with many others – one Gentleman left the Room; when the others disputing what his Profession could be & referring themselves to the Doctor – "'I do not like says he to traduce any Man – but I suspect he is an Attorney.'" – perhaps this was mentioned before.

Garrick Takes Umbrage ↬ Mr Johnson being told that Garrick took umbrage at not being mentioned in His edition of Shakespear: why what is it to me says he as Editor of Shakespear, that Mr Garrick can mouthe a Tragedy, – or skip a Comedy?

Garrick's Feelings ↬ Garrick* was one night coming on the Stage in Lear as I remember, when Johnson laughing or arguing behind the Scenes made such a Noise that the little Man was teized by it – and said at last – do have done with all this Rattle. – it spoyls my Thoughts, it destroys my *Feelings* – No No Sir returns the other – (loud enough for all the players to hear him) – I know better things – *Punch* has no *feelings*.

IV DAVID GARRICK
*Engraved by Evans, after a painting by
Sir Joshua Reynolds*

Garrick as 'Prospero' ↢ I have heard that the Character of Prospero in the Rambler was written as a Portrait for Garrick, & Johnson himself says that Garrick believes it & has never forgiven him, tho' they live upon Terms of Friendship: I know he thinks extremely well of Mr Garrick's Beneficence of which nobody could be a better Judge because he was perpetually begging Money of all his rich Acquaintance for Purposes of Charity; which says he is one of the Thousand Reasons for keeping up a Connection with Life.

The Profession of Actor ↢ For his Profession as an Actor he had however no Reverence, nor any great Fondness for the Stage I think: it was of the Play called Barbarossa that he observed how the Author had rung a Bell among the Turks where there are no Bells merely to imitate Otway's Contrivance of impressing the Audience with Terror, as if says he Men were to be made April Fools twice by the same Trick.

Mrs Johnson ↢ Mr Johnson has told me sometimes that his Wife read Comedy better than ever he heard anybody – in Tragedy he said I did better, She always mouthed too much.

I asked him once whether he ever disputed with his Wife (I knew he adored her) Oh Yes perpetually my dear says he; She was extremely neat in her disposition, & always fretful that I made the House so dirty – a clean Floor is *so* comfortable she would say by way of twitting; till at last I told her, I thought we had had Talk enough about the Floor, we would now have a Touch at the *Cieling*.

On some other Occasion he mentioned his Wife and said She had the Fault of shewing every one the bad Side of their own Profession – Situation &c. would lament the Sorrows of Celibacy to an old Maid, & once told a Waterman he was no happier than a Galley Slave – one was chained to the

Oar by Authority She said, & the other by Want.

Importance of Dinner ↜ Johnson loved his Dinner extremely, and has often said in my hearing, and for my Edification I guess – that where the Dinner is ill gotten, the Family is somehow grossly wrong: there is Poverty or there is Stupidity says he; for a Man seldom thinks much more earnestly of anything than of his Dinner, and if he cannot get that well done, he should be suspected of Inaccuracy in other Things: Upon this I one day asked him if he ever huffed his Wife about his meat? Yes Yes replied he, but then She huffed me worse; for She said one Day as I was going to say Grace – Nay hold says She, and do not make a Farce of thanking God for a Dinner which you will presently protest not eatable.

Johnson's Wedding Day ↜ The Account of his Wedding day was comical enough: I was riding to Church says Johnson & She following upon another single Horse – She hung back however, & I turned about to see whether She could get her Steed along, or what was the matter: but I had soon occasion to observe it was Coquettery only & that I despised, so mending *my* Pace She mended hers, but I believe there was a Tear or two – Pretty dear Creature!

A Little Painted Poppet ↜ Garrick says the Woman was a little painted Poppet; full of Affectation and rural Airs of Elegance; old Levett says She was always drunk & reading Romances in her Bed, where She killed herself by taking Opium: Her Daughter shewed me her Picture which was pretty, & as She was a Widow with Children I rather think She must have been in most respects a Woman quite like her Neighbours, but that her second Choice made her a Person to enquire about.

The Education of Children ↘ If you had had Children say'd I to him one day, would you have taught them any thing? I would replied he have lived on Bread & Water that they might learn, but I would not have had them about me; Boarding Schools are made to relieve Parents from that anxiety which only torments them: A Man & his Wife cannot agree which Child to fondle, nor how to fondle them; so they put them to School, & remove the Cause of Contention – Strahan & his Lady added he are a good proof of all this: the little Girl pokes her head, the Mother reproves her the Father says My dear don't mind your Mama but do your own Way – Mrs Strahan complains to me on't: Madam says I your Husband is right enough: he is with you two hours in the Day only; & then you torment him with making the Girl cry – Is not ten hours sufficient for you to tutor her? – put her to School however, & have done; tis better She were away than you should quarrel.

A Low View of Women ↘ Mr Johnson was always of the Men's Side when there was a domestick Dispute: Ld Abergavenny turned his Lady – a Woman of Birth – out of doors after 14 Years Cohabitation & took in the Nursery Maid who was set at the Head of the Table: why says the Doctor I doubt not but it was the Lady's Fault; Women often give great Offence by their Spirit of Non Compliance: their Husband wants them to sit in the Shade, & then they feel earnest desire to walk in the Sun; he offers to read to her & She rings for the Children to make a Noise & disturb him – twenty such Tricks will a Woman play & then be astonished that the Man fetches in a Mistress.

He had indeed a very ill opinion of the Sex in general, A Woman says he is the proper Person to do Business, the Men smooth the way for her as they would not for each other, and besides She never stops for Integrity.

Life Must Be Filled Up ↝ The vacuity of Life had at some early Period of his Life perhaps so struck upon the Mind of Mr Johnson, that it became by repeated Impression his favourite hypothesis, & the general Tenor of his reasonings commonly ended in that. The Things therefore which other Philosophers attribute to various & contradictory Causes, appeared to him uniform enough; all was done to fill up the Time upon his Principle. one Man for example was profligate, followed the Girls or the Gaming Table, – why Life *must* be filled up Madam, & the Man was capable of nothing less Sensual. Another was active in the management of his Estate & delighted in domestick Œconomy: Why a Man *must do something*, & what so easy to a narrow Mind as hoarding halfpence till they turn into Silver? a Third was conspicuous for maternal Tenderness, and spent her Youth in caressing or instructing her Children – Enquire however before you commend, cries he; & you will probably perceive that either her want of health or Fortune prevented her from tasting the Pleasures of the World: I once talked to him of a Gentleman who loved his Friend – he has nothing else to do replies Johnson; Make him prime Minister, & see how long his Friend will be remembered.

Money & Mops ↝ Little Mr Evans of Southwark had preached one Sunday, & being struck with the Discourse I commended it to our Doctor, what was it about said he? Friendship reply'd I. ""and what does the blockhead preach about Friendship in a busy Place like this where no one can ever be thinking of it."" Why what are they *thinking* of said I, why the Men replied Johnson are thinking of their Money, & the Women are thinking of their Mops.

Busy People ↝ High Rank escaped no better; when Lady Tavistock died for Grief at the Loss of her Husband,* how

I pity her said somebody! so do not I answered Johnson; She was rich and wanted Employment, so She cried till She lost the Power of restraining her tears: putting her into a small Shop, & giving her a Nurse Child to tend would have saved her Life now, – Busy People are never strongly affected with Grief.

One of my own Children was ill & I fretted to see my husband so very little affected – you says Mr Johnson may make a stir about Lucy's Teeth for you have nothing else to make a stir about, but he has his Great Casks to fill.

Idleness ↭ As Idleness is apt to give opportunities for the Cultivation of that Sensibility which is always blunted by Employment, so says he it nurses all evil and prurient Passions; and it is upon this Principle that Mr Johnson recommends Dissipation to those who are but poorly supplied with intellectual Entertainment, & persists to maintain against all Opposition that the more young Ladies are in Publick the Safer they are; for where says he can Virtue be so certainly secured as under the inspection of hundreds? each Individual is in a Place of publick Amusement a useful Spy upon his Neighbour's Prudence, & no harm can be done before so many Witnesses.

Danger of Solitude ↭ Solitude adds he is dangerous even to the old & wise, how then shall the young resist its powerful Temptations? Life is a Pill which cannot be swallowed without gilding, & if tumultuous Pleasures are refused us, we shall recur to those of mere Appetite; for the solicitations of Sense are always at hand, & a Dram to a vacant & Solitary Person is a seducing Relief. Remember, would he continue, that the solitary Mortal, is certainly luxurious, probably superstitious, and possibly mad: the mind stagnates for want of Employment; grows morbid, & is extinguished like a Candle in foul Air.

Reject No Positive Good ∽ There was another Tenet of our Doctor's well worth recording: Reject says he to somebody no positive Good: the Spirit of such rejection proceeds only from a mean Affectation of the Power to penetrate Consequences: – thus a Man of this Character will not marry a Wife of high Birth lest her Pride should prove offensive, and is afraid of a Beauty lest she should expose him by Coquetry: My *prudent* Friend therefore picks up an Animal whose coarseness disgusts him, whose Ignorance distresses, and whose narrowness perplexes him; and thinks it amazing that so *dispassionate* a Choice produces so little Felicity: There is in Life says Mr Johnson so very little Felicity to be possessed with Innocence, that we ought surely to catch diligently all that can be had without the hazard of Virtue.

Thoughts on Education ∽ Something like this same Principle was always discoverable in Mr Johnson's thoughts on Education: he hated the cruel prudence by which Childhood is made miserable that Manhood may become insensible to Misery by frequent Repetition, yet no one more delighted in that general Discipline by which Children were restrained from tormenting their grown up friends, nor more despised the Imbecillity of Parents who are contented to profess their want of Power to govern: how says he is an Army governed? old People I have often heard him observe were very unfit to manage Children; for being most commonly idle themselves they filled up their Time as he said by tormenting the young Folks with Prohibitions not meant to be obeyed & Questions not intended to be answered. his own Parents had it seems teiz'd him so to exhibit his Knowledge &c. to the few Friends they had, that he used to run up a Tree when Company was expected, that he might escape the Plague of being show'd off to them.

His Indulgence to Children ↶ He was in his Turn extremely indulgent to Children, not because he lov'd them, for he loved them not, but because he feared extremely to disoblige them: a Child says he is capable of resentment much earlier than is commonly suppos'd, & I never could endure my Fathers Caresses after he had once rendered them displeasing to me by mingling them with Caresses I did not care to comply with.

Old People Have No Honour ↶ As he was always on the side of the husband against the Wife, so he was always on the side of the Children against the Old ffolks – old People says he have no Honour, no Delicacy; the World has blunted their Sensibility & Appetite or Avarice governs the last Stage.

This was our talk one Morning at Breakfast, when a favourite Spaniel stole our Muffin which stood by the Fire to keep hot; – Fye Belle said I you used to be upon honor, Yes Madam replied Johnson – but *Belle grows old*.

Belle the Spaniel ↶ Of the same Spaniel when She teized him at Dinner he once said; this Dog would have been a fit member of the Society established by Lycurgus, She condemns one to a State of perpetual Vigilance.

Johnson's Manners ↶ Although M[r] Johnson would say the roughest, and most cruel Things he always wished for the Praise of good Breeding, which however he did not obtain except from D[r] Barnard* who once asserted – I know not why – that Johnson was the civillest person in the World: true it is, that he was more ceremonious than many Men; he would not sit forward or on your right hand in a Coach, tho' he would take up so much room in it you could not sit yourself; he would not go to dinner till you arrived if he was ever so hungry, or the Hour ever so late; would not displace

[36]

an Infant if sitting in the Chair he chose, & always said he was more attentive to others than any body was to him – & yet says he *People call me rude*.

His Friends ∽ Of all his intimates and Friends, I think I never could find any who much loved him Boswell & Burney excepted – Mr Murphy too loved him as he loves People – when he sees them – All the others would rather not have seen him than seen him as far as I have been able to observe; & as to Burney had they been more together, they would have liked each other less; but I who delighted greatly in them both, used to keep those Parts of their Characters out of Sight wch would have offended the other. This was a mighty easy Operation to me; & I grew skilful in it by long Practice; nor was it in itself difficult, as Mr Johnson's great Deficiency both in Sight & Hearing put him so far in one's power.

Mrs Salusbury ∽ My Mother* & he did not like one another much the first two or three Years of their Acquaintance; the Truth was each thought I loved the other better than I needed; as both however were excellent people, they grew insensibly to have great friendship; & nothing could be more solemn or striking than his last Leave of her on the fatal eighteenth of June 1773. when I called him to her Deathbed, & he feeling her Pulse observed it did not yet intermit; but seeing the too visible Alteration in her Countenance, and drawing still nearer, he gave her the final Kiss; & said in his peculiarly emphatick manner; "'God bless you dearest Madam! for Jesus Christ's sake, and receive your Soul to Salvation!'"

I can write no more just now! I will go on with Johnson on the other side.

On Convents ○ The Piety of Doctor Johnson was exemplary & edifying; yet he had none of that Turn to religious Mortifications which the Roman Catholick votaries to Virtue are apt enough to practise. when we were abroad together I used to talk with him of the hardships suffered in Places of Seclusion: remember says he that Convents are *idle* Places of Course, & where nothing can be *done*, something must be *suffered*, or the insipidity of Monastic Life would produce Madness: Mustard has a bad Taste, but you cannot eat *Brawn* without it. – Of the Claires, Carthusians &c. he used to say that they should write upon their Gates what Dante writes upon the Gates of Hell;

    Lasciate ogni Speranza – voi ch'entrate.*

The Highest Exercise of Reason ○ Religion adds Johnson, is the highest Exercise of Reason; let us not begin it by turning all reason out of Doors. – I would tell him too sometimes that his Morality was easily satisfied, & when I have lamented to him the wickedness of the World – he has often answer'd – Prythee my Dearest let us have done with Canting, there is very little of gross Iniquity to be seen; & still less of extraordinary Virtue.

Life Made Up of Little Things ○ Nothing seemed to disgust Johnson so greatly as Hyperbole; he loved not to hear of Sallies of Excellence; Heroick Virtues said he one day are the bons Mots of Life, they seldom appear & are therefore when they do appear – much talked of,† but Life is made up of little Things, & that Character is best which does little, but continued Acts of Beneficence; as that Conversation is the best which consists in little, but elegant & pleasing Thoughts; expressed in easy, natural and pleasing Terms.

 † How like all this is to J: J: Rousseau who says – Je ferois un Roman tout comme un autre, mais la Vie n'est point un Roman.*

[38]

Notions of Moral Virtue ∽ With Regard to my Notions of moral Virtue, I hope I have not lost my Sensibility of Wrong, but I hope likewise that I have seen sufficient of the World to prevent my expecting to find any Action whose Motives, & all its Parts are good. This last expression fell from him this day.

Stains of Corruption ∽ He had in his Youth been a great Reader of Mandeville, and was very watchful for the Stains of original Corruption both in himself & others – I mentioned an Event which might have greatly injured Mr Thrale once! & said – if it had happened now said I – how sorry you would have been! – I *hope* replies he gravely, & after a Pause – that I should have been *very* sorry.

A Foolish Rascal ∽ He was indeed no great sorrower for Events he had himself no Share in; I told him one Day of an Acquaintance who had hanged himself – he was an old Beau – Foolish Rascal says Johnson – why he had better have been airing his Clothes.

Mrs Boothby & Dr Bathurst ∽ Baretti says his Concern for the Loss of Mrs Boothby* whom he loved with great Attachment lasted but a Week, & when Dr Bathurst died; whom he professed to love beyond all mortals when I knew him first – I saw no extraordinary Emotion – I believe however now I think on't, he was dead before I knew Mr Johnson.

A Good Hater ∽ Bathurst says he to'ther day – was a fine Fellow! he hated a Fool, & he hated a Rogue, & he hated a Whig – He was a very good Hater!

His Tenderness for Poverty ∽ Mr Johnson has more Tender-

[39]

ness for Poverty than any other Man I ever knew; and less for other Calamities: the person who loses a Parent Child or Friend he pities but little – these says he are the Distresses of Sentiment – which a Man who is *indeed* to be pitied – has no leisure to feel: the want of Food & Raiment is so common in London adds Johnson, that one who lives there has no Compassion to spare for the Wounds given only to Vanity or Softness.

In consequence of these Principles he has *now* in his house whole Nests of People who would if he did not support them be starving I suppose:–

A Blind woman* & her Maid, a Blackamoor and his Wife, a Scotch Wench* who has her Case as a Pauper depending in some of the Law Courts; a Woman* whose Father once lived at Lichfield & whose Son is a strolling Player, – and a superannuated Surgeon* to have Care of the whole *Ship's Company*. such is the present State of Johnson's Family resident in Bolt Court – an Alley in Fleet Street, which he gravely asserts to be the best Situation in London; and thither when he is at home he keeps a sort of odd Levee for distress'd Authors, breaking Booksellers, & in short every body that has even the lowest Pretensions to Literature in Distress.

Mean while he has a Cousin at Coventry who is wholly maintained by him and a Female Cousin a Mrs Herne I forget where to whom he regularly remits 10$^£$ a Year, & She is I think his cheapest Dependant.

Making A Bargain ↝ Mr. Johnson has of Course ways enough to spend his Income which he is willing to increase by doing now & then a Job for Booksellers; & I believe few People know better how to make their Bargain – for says he I do not love to beat down the price of Learning.

V THE SITTING ROOM AT BOLT COURT

Prefaces & Dedications ∽ His Friends often prevailed on him to write Prefaces, Dedications &c. for them, but he did not love it – one would rather says he one Day give anything than that which one is used to sell, Would not you Sir – to Mr Thrale – rather give a Man Money than Porter.

The Doctor however was no good refuser, and you might coax him out of any thing except out of a Visit, which I think he has been very backward in paying of late Years, unless he is asked to Dinner.

The Poor ∽ But to return to his Notions concerning the Poor; he really loved them as nobody else does – with a Desire they should be happy – What signifies says somebody giving Money to common Beggars? they lay it out only in Gin or Tobacco – and why should they not says our D^r why should every body else find Pleasure necessary to their Existence and deny the poor every possible Avenue to it? – Gin & Tobacco are the only Pleasures in their Power, – let them have the Enjoyments within their reach without Reproach.

Coarse Pleasures ∽ Mr Johnson's own Pleasures – except those of Conversation – were all coarse ones: he loves a good Dinner dearly – eats it voraciously, & his notions of a good Dinner are nothing less than delicate – a Leg of Pork boyl'd till it drops from the bone almost, a Veal Pye with Plumbs & Sugar, & the outside Cut of a Buttock of Beef are his favourite Dainties, though he loves made Dishes Soups &c: sowces his Plumb Pudden with melted Butter, & pours Sauce enough into every Plate to drown all Taste of the Victuals.

His Drinking Habits ∽ With regard to Drink his liking is for the *strongest*, as it is not the Flavour but the Effect of Wine which he even professes to desire, and he used often to pour

Cappillaire into his Glass of Port when it was his Custom to drink Wine which he has now left wholly off: To make himself amends for this Concession, he drinks Chocolate liberally, & puts in large Quantities of Butter or of Cream: he loves Fruit exceedingly, & though I have seen him eat of it immensely, he says he never had his Bellyful of Fruit but twice – once at our House and once at Ombersly the Seat of my Lord Sandys.

Luxuries of Porridge Island ↬ I was saying this Morning that I did not love Goose much one smells it so says I – But you Madam replies Johnson have always had your hunger forestalled by Indulgence, & do not know the Pleasure of smelling one's Meat before hand: – a Pleasure answered I that is to be had in Perfection by all who walk through *Porridge Island* of a Morning! – come come says the Doctor gravely, let us have done laughing at what is serious to so many: Hundreds of your Fellow Creatures dear Lady turn another way that they may not be tempted by the Luxuries of *Porridge Island*† to hope for Gratifications they are not able to obtain.

These Notions – just as they doubtless are; – seem to me the fæculancies of his low Birth, which I believe has never failed to leave its *Stigma* indelible in every human Creature; however exalted by Rank or polished by Learning: – no Varnish though strong can totally cover primæval meanness, nor can any Situation of Life remove it out of the Sight even of a cursory & casual Observer.

The Manners of a Gentleman ↬ As no Man better liked to be

---

† *Porridge Island* is an Alley in Cov.t Garden between Chandois Street & the Strand, where there are numbers of ordinary Cooks Shops to supply the low working People with Meat at all hours. Beef – Pudden Pig & particularly Goose: the whole Court has by its Smell and its Fame obtained the proper Appellation of *Porridge Island*.

genteely Complimented than Johnson, so no Man ever had the power of Complimenting with a better Grace; for he always contrived to raise the Person he commended without lowering himself.

It is however some what remarkable that no Flattery was so welcome to him, as that which told him he had the Mind or Manners of a *Gentleman*, which he always said was the most complete & the most difficult to obtain: one said an Officer had commonly the Manner of a Gentleman; on the contrary says Johnson he is generally branded very deeply with the mark of his Profession, now 'tis the Essence of A Gentleman's Character to have no professional Mark whatever. – An Officer added he is seldom *bright* indeed, but he is almost always *smooth*. Talking on upon this Subject, he nam'd Mr Berenger as particularly elegant in his Carriage and Behaviour, but on my objecting his resemblance to the Gentlemen in Congreve's Comedies, and that he rather seemed to *play* the Man of Fashion than to *be* it, he changed him for Tom Hervey who is dead & gone, and was doubtless as completely a Gentleman as one shall ever know.

Mr Johnson used to say that bright Parts were like Gold, common Sense like Iron, but more of this in the Idler:

The Idler ∽ The Idlers came out without his name to them, & without Mottoes; he talks of publishing them sometime with Mottoes and bid me chuse proper ones; I did fit about 20 Numbers in some Humour, & wrote them on a Card which I have now lost, and so the Scheme like many a greater, dropt to nothing.

Visiting the Chartreuse ∽ Here is another of his Schemes which will fall to nothing: my heart says he yesterday is set upon seeing the Chartreuse in company with my Mistress; – we *will* go sometime that's certain, then replied I – whose

Heart is set on very different Projects – we must write Verses to leave behind us; well returned he few People's Verses will be better than ours, we need not stay at home for want of *poetical* Powers: but are you willing to go? No Sir said I gravely: are you unwilling? Yes Sir, – in the same Accent: then says he I'll work up my Master to make you go, for go we will.

Johnson as Travelling Companion ↜ Johnson was in some Respects a very good Travelling Companion: The Rain, & the Sun, the night and the Day were the same to him, and he had no Care about Food, Hours or Accomodations; but then he expected that nobody else should have any neither, and felt no sort of Compassion for one's Fatigue, or uneasiness, or Confinement in the Carriage – for nobody ever talks of such Stuff says he, except the People who have nothing else to say, & if one *said* nothing – why 'tis because you *feel* nothing to be sure says he.

The Club ↜ Mr Johnson had ever since I knew him an enthusiastick fondness for Poetry, indeed for all sorts of Literature; and had a respect for a Club* he belonged to, that was little less than ridiculous; our Club Madam said he is a Society which can scarcely be matched in the World – we have Reynolds for Painting, Goldsmith for Poetry, Percy for Antiquities, Nugent for Physick; Chamiere for Trade, Politics and all Money Concerns; Mr Burke for Oratory, Mr Beauclerck for Polite Literature, Dyer for Modern History & Travels, Chambers for the Law, Langton for Ecclesiastical History & indeed all Branches of Learning Sir John Hawkins for Judicature & ancient Musick. – I have forgotten the other Members & his Eulogiums upon them; but many are dead, & new Members have come in – I suppose against his Consent – for he now says the Club is spoyl'd.

Modern Poetry ∽ He had however no Taste for Modern Poetry – Gray Mason &c. – Modern Poetry says he one day at our house, is like Modern Gardening, every thing now is raised by a hot bed; every thing therefore is forced, & everything tasteless.

One may therefore without much difficulty conceive, how his Friend Grierson must have offended him when he observed that a Cook was a more excellent & useful Being than a Poet: Ay replies Johnson, and in that Opinion – all the Dogs in the Town will join with you.

A Gardening Book ∽ A propós to Gardening he once advised me to buy myself some famous Book upon the Subject, and read it says he – attentively, but do not believe it; use the World likewise as a large book, but use it with the same Restriction.

Cruelty to Mrs Langton ∽ One cannot be sorry for the Rebuff given to Grierson but it was cruel to Mrs Langton when she shewed him her Grotto, & asked if he did not think it a pretty convenient habitation? – Yes Madam replied he – for a Toad.

Examples of Rudeness ∽ The Abbé Renard or Reinel* I forget his Name who had published some Infidel Writings – was at a house and in a Room with Johnson – I think it was Paradice's; Sir says the Master of the Family will you permit me to introduce to you the Abbé Reinel – he had the Man in his hand too – *No Sir* replies the Doctor, & turns away in a Huff.

In the same Spirit – when young Cholmondeley rode up to our Carriage as we drove through Derbyshire – Mr Thrale – seeing him address Johnson in a Style civilly familiar, & knowing them to be acquainted; – tapped the D^r who was reading, & said Sir, that is Mr Cholmondeley, – well Sir replies Johnson raising His Eyes from the Book, – and *what if it is* Mr Cholmondeley!

His Strength ∽ Mr Johnson's bodily Strength & Figure has not yet been mentioned; his Heighth was five Foot eleven without Shoes, his Neck short, his Bones large & His Shoulders broad: his Leg & Foot eminently handsome, his hand handsome too, in spite of Dirt, & of such Deformity as perpetual picking his Fingers necessarily produced: his Countenance was rugged, tho' many People pretended to see a benignity of Expression when he was in Good humour.

Garrick tells a Story how at a strolling Play in some Country Town, a young Fellow took away Johnson's Chair which he had quitted for five minutes; & seated himself in it on the Stage: when the original Possessor returned, he desired him to leave his Chair which he refused, & claimed it as his own: Johnson did not offer to dispute the Matter, but lifting up Man & Chair, and all together in his Arms, took & threw them at one Jerk into the Pit.

Beauclerck's Pointers ∽ Beauclerck tells a Story of him that he had two large Pointers brought into the Parlour on some Occasion to shew his Company and they immediately fastening on one another alarmed the People present not a little with their ferocity, till Johnson gravely laying hold on each Dog by the Scuft of the Neck, held them asunder at Arms length, and said come Gentlemen where is your difficulty? put one of them out at one Door & t'other out of the other; & let us go on with our Conversation. – he confirmed these two Stories himself to me before I would write them down.

I saw him myself once throw over a Bathing Tub full of

Water, which two of the Footmen had tryed in vain to overturn, but says he these Fellows have no more strength than Cats.

Johnson's Jump ∽ As an Instance of his Activity I will only mention, that one day after riding very hard for fifty Miles after Mr Thrales Foxhounds – they were sitting and talking over the Chase when Dinner was done in our blue Room at Streatham; I mentioned some Leap they spoke of as difficult; no more says Johnson than leaping over that Stool – it was a Cabriolet that stood between the Windows – which says I, would not be a very easy Operation to you I believe after fifty Miles Galloping – & in Boots too. he said no more, but jumped fairly over it, & so did Mr Thrale who is however full twenty Years younger than the Doctor.

A Time and A Place ∽ Johnson loved a Frolick or a Joke well enough, tho he had strange serious Rules about them too, and very angry was he always at poor me for being merry at improper times and Places – You care for nothing says he, so you can crack your Joke –

One Day to be sure I was saucy in that way & he was very much affronted: my friend Mrs Strickland and he were entered into a Dispute whose Dress was most expensive – a Gentleman's or a Lady's. Mrs Strickland instanced Lady Townsend's Extravagance, & said She knew of her having a new Cloke of eight Guineas Value every three Months – a Cloke Madam! cries Johnson, & was going to make a serious Answer; why Lord bless me what does a Young Girl marry an old Lord *for* said I – but for a *Cloke*? he did not like to be served so.

Harold Harefoot ∽ In the same manner when a foolish Fellow had fretted him one day at Chester; shewing him the Curiosities of the place, & yet running from Thing to thing, so that he had no Time to see any distinctly – what is this Gentleman's Name says Johnson to me gravely, his Name is Harold I understand replied I, and I fancy for my Part that we should call him *Harold Harefoot*. That Joke is so good says the Doctor that you are Glad he has plagued us so – to bring it in.

Love of Numbers ↶ Mʳ Johnson had a consummate Knowledge of Figures and an uncommon delight in Arithmetical Speculations; he had too a singular Power of withdrawing his Attention from the prattle he heard round him, and would often sit amusing himself with calculating Sums while there was a Noise in the room enough to perplex any common Mortal, & prevent their Thinking at all.

He used indeed to be always tormenting one with shewing how much Time might be lost by squandering two hours a day, how much Money might be saved by laying up five Shillings a day, how many Lines might be written by putting down only ten every day with a hundred such like Propositions.

An Odd Calculation ↶ One Time that he was greatly indisposed at our house with the Spasms in his Stomach, which tormented him so long; he found himself unable to bear Company – so sat alone in the next Room, & made an odd Calculation: no other than that the National Debt, setting it at 130 Millions Sterling would, if converted into Silver make a Meridian of that metal for the real Globe of the Earth. – this might be called the *Meridian* of *London* very properly.

Soame Jennings Refuted ↶ I mentioned to him one day Soame Jennings's* Refutation of Paschal, as thus;†

† I remember this Conversation passed in the Coach as we were airing one Day between Brighthelmston and Rottenden, I think in the Year 1769.

[49]

Infinity – says the French Geometrician – tho' on all sides astonishing, is most so when connected with numbers; for the Idea of infinite Number – & infinite number we know *there is* – can hardly find room in the human Mind, but stretches it still more than the Idea of infinite Space. Our English Philosopher on the other hand exclaims; – I mean Soame Jennings – Let no man give his tongue leave to talk of infinite Number, for infinite Number is a Contradiction in Terms; if [it] is Numbered, it is not infinite I'll warrant it. What do *you* say to these contenders Mr Johnson? – why *I* say replied he, that *Numeration* is infinite, for Eternity might be employed in adding Figure to Figure, or if you will better comprehend me – Unit to Unit; but each Number is *finite*, which the possibility of doubling it easily proves; besides, stop where you will; you will find yourself as far from Infinitude as ever. – So much for his Arithmetick.

Scruples ∽ With regard to Virtue I can only say that he was uniformly, not capriciously good; nor thought it right to load Life with unnecessary Scruples.

Scruples says he seldom make a Man good, but they certainly make him miserable. He had however very piously and judiciously scrupled among the various Authorities he quotes in his Dictionary ever to give one from an immoral or an Infidel Writer, lest says he the Quotation should send People to look in an Author that might taint their Virtue, or poyson their Principles.

More than Forty Frenchmen ∽ Somebody complimented Mr Johnson on his Dictionary, & said he had done more than forty Frenchmen, why what could you expect replied he, from Fellows that eat Frogs? – I dare say this is mentioned before, but I write from Memory, & can neither recollect every Trifle, nor turn back to see whether 'tis down or no.

Mr Hunter of Stourbridge ◦∽ I know not whether I put it into this Book or no, but Johnson always hated his Schoolmaster – a Mr Hunter of Stourbridge I think his name was and I have heard him say that the hatred was reciprocal.

He left that Hunter at the Age of 18: and spent a Year at Oxford where he felt, I find; and I am sure he *expressed*, most sovereign Contempt for his Instructors.

His Political Opinions ∽ I must here have a Stroke at his Political Opinions, though God knows he has not left them dubious till *now*. He is a Tory in what he calls the truest sense of the Word; and is strongly attached to the notion of Divine & Hereditary Right inherent in Kings: he was therefore a *Jacobite* while *Jacob* existed, or any of his Progeny was likely to sit on the Throne: he is now however firmly attached to the present Royal Family; not from change of Principles, but difference of Situations, and he is as zealous that *this* King should maintain his Prerogatives, as if he belonged to the exiled Family.

Aversion to Whigs ∽ His Aversion to a Presbyterian is great, to a consistent, Whig as he often calls a Deist, 'tis still greater, we mentioned Alderman Trecothic's having behaved odly on some Occasion: is he not a Citizen of London, a Native of N: America, a *Whig* says Mr Johnson? let him be absurd I beg of you, when a Monkey is *too* like a Man he shocks one.

Canting ∽ A Contempt for small Matters – & he thinks few great – is however a Characteristick of Mr Johnson in all Things – Politics not excepted; so that now the popular Clamour runs so high about our Disgraces in America,† our Debt at home, our Terrors of a Bankruptcy, & Fears of a French War; what signifies all this Canting says the Doctor?

† The Capitulation of Burgoyne & his whole Army in the Year 1777.

the World goes on just as it did; who eats the less? or who sleeps the worse? or where is all this *Consternation* you talk of – but in the News papers. Nobody is thinking or feeling about the matter, otherwise than 'tis somewhat to talk about.

Character of a Statesman ↝ I was one Day exalting the Character of a Statesman, & expatiating on the Skill required to direct the different departments, reconcile the jarring Interests &c. – Thus replies Mr Johnson a *Mill* is a curious Construction enough, but the Water is no part of the Workmanship.

Jerry Sneyd & Tom Cotton ↝ I was in another Humour lamenting how all publick Business was left to Clerks – Jerry Sneyd sayd I & Tom Cotton – pretty Fellows to have any Direction in State Affairs; you may as well answered he complain that the Account of Time should be kept by the Clock; for to be sure he is no considerable Chronologer.

Lord Chatham ↝ Of the Conduct of Lord Chatham he observed the other day, that Ambition in its last ramifications ends in Vanity, as an Old Oak at last puts forth nothing but Twigs & Leaves.

Licentious Times ↝ Apropos to Johnson's contempt of Trifles – in November 1769 a female Servant in Our house was suspected of murdering her Bastard; the same Day Baretti was taken up for killing a Man in the Streets, our Gentlemen were running from Coroner to Coroner, when Seward observed how licentious the Times were grown, for see now says he, if the Bird catchers be not out tho' tis Sunday. – since this Speech was made I hardly ever dare lament Distresses of which the Consequences are at least distant, if not uncertain; for if I do, Mr Johnson is sure to remind me of the Iniquity of catching Birds on a Sunday.

John Wilkes ↝ Party Matters run very high however in the beginning of the Year 1770. Johnson wrote his False Alarm* at our House in the Borough that February of a Wednesday Night & Thursday Night which was all the Time he bestowed on it to my certain Knowledge.

I heard one Day in the Year 1775 I think when Wilkes was Mayor however; that he expressed his Desire of Dr Johnson's Company at the Mansion house to eat Turtle with him forsooth; 'Tis a liberal Fellow said I in spite of his Principles, & a genteel Fellow in spite of his mean Birth: He *is* a fine Fellow replies Mr Johnson, but let us remember that it would be a triumph to Wilks, to shew me that he is just where King Lords and Commons and myself forsooth, have all endeavoured to prevent him from being.

Burke's Speech ↝ It was in the same Year 1775 that I was venturing to praise Mr Burke's famous Speech,* especially that Passage of Lord Bathurst and the Angel, which said Mr Johnson had I been in the house I would have answered thus: ""Suppose Mr Speaker, that to Wharton or to Marlborough, or some of the most eminent Whigs in the last Age – the Devil, had – not with any great Impropriety consented to appear; – He would perhaps in these Words have commenced the Conversation.

""You seem my Lord to be concerned at the judicious Apprehension; that while you are sapping the Foundations of Royalty, and propagating the Doctrines of Resistance here at home, the Distance of America may secure its Inhabitants from your Arts though active; but I will unfold to you the gay Prospects of Futurity: this People now so innocent, so harmless, shall draw the Sword upon their Mother Country & bathe its Point in the Blood of their Benefactors: this People, now contented with a little; shall then refuse to spare what they themselves confess they could not miss; & these

Men, now so honest and so grateful shall in return for Peace & for Protection *fee their vile* Agents in the house of Parliament, there to sow the seeds of Sedition, & propagate Confusion Perplexity & Pain. Be not dispirited then at the Contemplation of their present happy State; I promise you that Anarchy Poverty & Death shall carry even across the spacious Atlantick – and settle even in America the Consequences of Whiggism.

A Young Whig & An Old Tory ∽ Johnson did not love telling Stories in Company but the following was one of his favourites; as it partly relates to Politics it shall come in here.

A Young Whiggish Gentleman in George the first's Time, went in to the Cocoa Tree, famous for being frequented by Tories; and calling for a Bowl of Punch, said to the Gentleman who sate next him Come Sir! here's Damn the Pope; and here's Damn the Pretender; and here's Damn the Devil too.

Sir says the old Tory cooly, permit me to make some Objections to your Toast: The Pope as a mere temporal Prince has Claims to *your* Respect I fancy, & if you care not for his Religion, you should at least pay some Deference to a Rank so high above your own: For the Pretender Sir he is Son to a Sovereign Prince, unfortunate indeed, but by no man supposed deserving of his Calamities, – but as to the *Devil* young Man look to yourself; for *he is my Friend* – abuse him now [who] dares.

Two of Johnson's Stories ∽ Here are however two more of Mr Johnsons Stories which have no Reference to Politics, as I have now done with that Stuff for the present.

When Mr Beauclerck & Mr Langton were going abroad together, they applied to their Banker for Money, to which he beg'd leave to add a Word or two of Advice; for Gentlemen says he do be careful of yourselves, & get into no Quarrels: this I grant will prove difficult, for I am told that a foreign Nobleman is so plaguy touchy – that if you *but shake your Stick at him*, he challenges you presently, be very cautious therefore among such kind of People.

The other was a Story how Tom Osborne the Bookseller had a Funeral Oration pronounced over some dowdy Daughter of his, setting forth how condescending She was to her Inferiors. this struck Mr Johnson who was well acquainted with the Wench, more than perhaps it did the Auditors either of the Sermon or of the Joke.

Tom Osborne ∽ I asked him the other day about his Combat with that Osborne,* how much of the Story was true: It was true said he that I beat the fellow, & that was all; but the World so hated poor Osborne; that they have never done multiplying the blows, and increasing the weight of them for twenty Years together; The Blockhead told the Story himself too originally, for I am sure I should not, – but says Osborne Johnson beat me this Morning in my own house – For what says his Friend – why for telling him that he *lied* forsooth.

In Vino Veritas? ∽ Mr Boswell however is the Man for a Johnsoniana: he really knows ten Times more Anecdotes of his Life than I do who see so much more of him; one thing however that passed between them at our own house – I must needs record.

Mr Boswell in order to induce Johnson to drink, expatiated on the praises of Wine: I know no good it does says Johnson, Yes replies the other, it makes a Man eloquent – Sir it makes him noisy & absurd: Boswell went on – & defeated in every point at last cry'd out – This you must allow – it makes a Man speak Truth: Sir says Johnson, I see no good there is in that

[55]

neither, unless he is a Lyar when he is sober.

The Finest Prospect in the World ~ When Mrs Brooke upon her Return to England from Quebec* told Mr Johnson that the Prospect *up* the River Saint Lawrence was the finest in the World – but Madam says he, the Prospect *down* the River St Lawrence is I have a Notion the finest you ever saw.

Mr Rose Refuted ~ Mr Rose of Hammersmith* was contending with Johnson for the Preeminence of the Scots Writers over the English; He set up his Authors as Murphy says, and the other knocked them down like Ninepins: Rose at length – to make sure of Victory – named Ferguson on Civil Society, & praised the Book for being written in a new manner: I do not says Johnson perceive the Value of *this new* Manner, it is only, like Buckinger, who had no hands – & so wrote with his Toes.*

No Excellence in Swift ~ Doctor Delap praised Swift's Style; Mr Johnson was not in the humour to subscribe to its Excellence; the Doctor was beat from one of Swifts Performances to another – but says he you must allow that there are *strong Facts* in the Account of the four last Years of Queen Anne; Yes sure Sir returns Mr Johnson, and so there are in the ordinary of Newgates Account.

A Spider's Bowels ~ Dear Doctor! said he one Day to the same Gentleman who was lamenting his bad health & tender Bowels; do not like a Spider keep perpetually spinning thus out of thy own Bowels.

Medical Matters ~ Mr Johnson was however exceedingly attentive to his own health, and having studied Medcine pretty regularly I believe at some Period of his Life he was tempted no little to the sin of Quackery.

I was much struck with what he said t'other Day concerning the Gout: It seldom says he takes the Fort by a Coup de main, but turning the Siege into a Blockade – obliges it to surrender at Discretion.

On another Occasion – such a Lady is very ill said I; what help has She called in? enquired Mr Johnson Dr James said I – but what is her Disorder – nothing positive I answered but a gradual though gentle Decline – She will dye then I fear replied the D^r for though when a person is hurrying to the Grave upon full Speed – a Physician may give them a Turn; – yet if they keep on a regular & slow Pace, no Care can save them.

The Soft Passion ∽ As My Peace has never been disturbed by the *soft Passion*, so it seldom comes in my head to talk of it. – one day however after reading the odd Dissertation upon it in the Huetiana, I was led to ask Johnson his general Opinion concerning that which has been thought the Spring of so many strange Actions good & bad. As I perhaps might speak at the beginning of the Conversation in something like what he thought a contemptuous Accent, he replied: No Person Madam ever yet treated the Passion of Love with Contempt, except from Stupidity – or Disappointment – those who never were in Love never were happy – for Nature will vindicate her own Feelings, and revenge the Insults offered her – This however was only a Flight, & he soon settled to more comfortable Talk; and first of all agreed that there were three sorts of Love; the first is that well known Passion raised by Desire & always accompanied by it; the second that Love which is excited by Tenderness, and accompanied by Contempt, as the Love one has for Children – & even favourite Animals; the Third is that one feels for one's Friend; the Delight one has in his Company, the Pride one

[57]

shares in his Praises; the enthusiastic Partiality one has for all he does, and the Influence one suffers him to have over all ones other Passions. – this Love says he is accompanied by Vanity, and the vainest People are most susceptible of it.

So here! at least in the beginning of the Chat, is a Touch of Rousseau again; but how perfectly in the Spirit of the Eloise was all the Continuation when that frankness of Heart was spoken of, by which people are prompted to tell Intentions before hand; and to keep no Trifles lurking in the Mind, till they swell into Things of Bulk. – Such Tricks, say Johnson & Rousseau are apt to end in Evil for this Reason; that She who loves to be mysterious naturally, will soon provide to herself cause of Mystery; I used the word *She* because 'tis their Opinion too that Women, are more apt to be infected with this Disease of the Mind than Men are, which as it originates from narrowness, may very well happen – for Women's Minds are commonly like their Shapes, either screwed up to ridiculous Smallness, or else loosed out – to a *Squab*, in their own emphatical phrase.

Solitude the Nurse of Passion ↝ But I have not yet done with the resemblance between Johnson's Sentiments and those of Rousseau – in the Affair of Love too! but so it is, that they are both of opinion that Solitude is the Nurse of *this* as well as of every Passion, that in the Tumult of Company, & hurry of Preparation, a Girl has neither time nor Inclination to listen to tender Speeches, nor can She retain the remembrance of them in her Mind – The Ball, the Show are not the dangerous Things – no! tis the Tête à Tête, the private Friend, the kind Consoler, the constant Companion that is dangerous; the publick Lover is not to be feared.

Johnson carried this so far as to say that if you shut up any Man and Woman for six Months together, so as to make them derive all their Pleasures from each other, they would inevitably fall in Love; but if at the End of that Term you would throw each of them into Assemblies, & let them change Partners at Pleasure; they would soon forget their mutual Attachment, which nothing but the necessity of some Connection, & the vacuity of Life had caused; & it was therefore that Johnson generally insisted, that the most public Places are the safest for those whose Passions are easily inflam'd.

A Reverence for the World ↝ Mr Johnson was indeed very unjustly supposed to be a Lover of Singularity – a man particular in his notions, and difficult in his Morality – whereas no Man had ever so settled a reverence for the World, & its Opinions; nor was less captivated by new Modes of Behaviour or Innovations in the Conduct of Life:–

Cards, Dress, Dancing all found their Advocates in Johnson, who inculcated upon Principle the Cultivation of Arts which others reject as Luxuries, or consider as Superfluities – Somebody would say – Such a Lady never touches a Card – how then does She get rid of her Time says Johnson, does She drink Drams? Such a Person never suffers Gentlemen to buzz in his Daughter's Ears; who is to buzz in her Ears then? – the Footman! Such a one dresses particularly plain always – He thinks himself then of more importance than he is; if he forbears to carry the Badge of his Rank upon his Back – the World has no Business to be teized to find Reasons for Respecting a Man who will not declare his Situation by his Dress, and he must be content with the little Attention that will necessarily be paid him for his neglect.

A Ragged Footman ↝ We drank Tea at a House where the Plate was splendid, & the China elegant – the Footman waited however in a ragged Livery: as we came home I mentioned it: why ay says the Doctor you may shut Poverty out of the Door if you please; but the Jade will poke her pale Face in at the Window.

A Good Useful Body ∽ We breakfasted once at another awkward Place; the Lady of the House had been much praised to me by a Man I thought well of, so I wondered things were no better: Why they are well enough I think replies Johnson the Woman is [a] good useful Body in her way no doubt, & can I'll warrant you direct her Neighbours where to buy a little *run Tea* as well as possible; such People are unable to square the Circle indeed, but why should they be able? they do the common Offices of Life as well as they need to do; – few can benefit, and fewer can please.

Melancholy People Always Sensual ∽ Mr Johnson is of Opinion that Melancholy & otherwise insane People are always Sensual; the misery of their Minds naturally enough forces them to recur for Comfort to their Bodies. this Observation should have been among his medical ones, but it dropt from him but an hour ago so I wrote it immediately as it fell.

All Quarrels to be Avoided ∽ We were likewise talking today at Breakfast of Mr Shenstone's Rule for keeping up kindness between Lovers, Friends or Relations: some little Quarrel says he should now & then be kindled, that the Soul may feel her own elastick Force; & return to the beloved Object with renewed Delight: Why now what a pernicious Maxim this is cries Johnson, surely all Quarrels ought to be avoided as nobody can possibly tell where they will end; besides that lasting Detestation is often the Consequence of occasional Disgust; and that the Cup of Life is already sufficiently displeasing, without making it more bitter by a Dash of Resentment.

Setting an Example to the Servants ↭ Upon the same Principle, as he one day listened while I told somebody Dr Collier's method of keeping the Servants in humour with his favourite Dog; by seeming rough with the Creature himself on many Occasions, & even sometimes crying out – Why does nobody knock this Cur's brains out? – by the way of exciting their kindness &c. This is all Refinement now says Johnson – the Servants would kick the Dog when they had thus obtained a Sanction for their Severity; & I once chid my Wife for beating her Cat before the Maid, who will now said I treat Puss with Cruelty perhaps – and plead at last her Mistress's Example.

These are trifling Stories, but they serve to shew how well he understood the meanest Trifles relative to Life & Manners.

Mr Lyttelton ↭ Of Mr Lyttelton – now Lord Westcote he observed – that he had more Chaff than Grain in him; as every thing *indeed* says he which grows up to so prodigious a Length – has.

The Miss Pitcheses ↭ Of the Miss Pitcheses* – Young Ladies who were labouring hard at the great Work of Education under their Mother's Management – he said – Those Wenches are like Trees nailed to a Wall, but tis a good *Standard* at last bears the Fruit one can bear at one's Table.

The Law ↭ Of the Law says he one day when I declared against it, – Let us I beg of you – have no general Abuse; the Law is the last Result of Publick Wisdom, acting upon publick Experience.

Mr Greenville's Marriage ○ Of Mr Greenville's Marriage to Miss Stapylton, which was at one Time strongly reported; tho' his first Wife had been dead but a fortnight – Johnson said – why one would think you had never heard such a Thing; & the People in St Giles's always did it.

The Report was false & groundless, but his Answer was as good as if it had been true.

The Apple of Discord ○ A more elegant instance of his Wit must be given though it was a Compliment to myself; An Apple was one Day picked out of Jelly, & the Company disputed so violently† that I bid them take Care lest it should prove the Apple of Discord – Johnson handed it *to me*, & said if it were that Apple – it was rightly bestowed *on the fairest*.

An Anecdote Repeated ○ A Scotsman was commending the Town of Glasgow, I presume Sir said Johnson you have never yet seen Brentford. – this probably is down already – it happen'd before he had been in Scotland.

Dr Goldsmith's Opposition ○ Doctor Goldsmith's equally certain yet fruitless Opposition to Johnson in every Argument, used to remind me of these Verses in Berni –

> Il pover Uomo che non se n'era accorto
> Andava combattendo – ed era Morto.*

Dryden & Pope ○ Johnson said that it was prettily observed by Voltaire, how Dryden drove the old respectable Coach & Six, but Pope figur'd away in a new-fashioned highly-polished Chariot & Pair.

Thrale for Ever ○ At our last Election for Southwark, some

† Whether it was natural or Artificial.

[62]

VI HENRY THRALE

Fools were consulting whether Mr Thrale should have a Yellow Ribbon in his Hat – Nonsense! says Mr Johnson – he might as properly be bid to cry *Thrale for ever*.

No Time for Hats ∽ At the same Election an ordinary Fellow – a Hatter who was zealous for our Cause came suddenly up to Johnson and embracing him cried out – Ah Sir 'tis no Time now to mind making of *Hats*! I was frighted, & thought the Doctor would be embarrassed by this half-drunken Hero; – But he with the utmost presence of Mind made answer in the same gay Tone, No Sir – Hats are of no use to us now but to throw up in the Air & huzza with.

Little Whitaker ∽ Another Day of the Election, when one of the Voters wanted to come up to the House I was in – with Intelligence: he could not get up for the Crowd – so Mr Johnson set his broad Back to the Door, & reaching his Hand pull'd in little Whitaker as if he had been a Doll.

The Lyon's Teeth ∽ One said at Dinner that Thunder was an aweful Noise; Johnson observ'd that the consciousness of our Danger made us think it such: nay replied I but 'tis the Lightning – not the Thunder that is dangerous; – on the same Principle answered he you need not in a Desart fear the roaring of the Lyon; but the Lyon that roars we all know must have Teeth.

Elastick Dulness ∽ Of all Ignorance says Johnson, beware of *Scientifick* Ignorance; and of all Dullness keep clear from *elastick* Dulness; which rises to resist you – it is like kicking a Woolsack.

Hope a Bubble ∽ Urging one Day the well known Hypothesis of Happiness being placed in Hope rather than possession;

This said the Doctor is more subtle than true: We talk of the Pleasures of Hope, we feel those of Possession, and no Man in his Senses would change the last for the first; Hope is a Bubble which by a gentle Breath may be blown to a large Size, but a rough Blast bursts it at once; hope is an Amusement rather than a Good, & is adapted to none but very tranquil Minds.

Vansittart & the Mouse ∽ Vansittart* had been talking a long Time about a Mouse; what says Johnson would Vansittart have said if he had seen a Lyon?

Lord Sandys's Marriage ∽ When the present Lord Sandys – despairing of his Fathers Death – married an ugly old Woman for her Money, He will now says Johnson get seven Dinners a Week, with the use of a Parlour; & for this the silly Dog like his Cousin in the Fable, will suffer his Neck to be galled with a Collar.

Johnson's Dread of Spirits ∽ Johnson was observing the other Day – He & I were alone – that almost every body had some particular Terror – some favourite Fear – as he called it – either of Thieves, or Fire, or Mad Dogs or something – *I have none* said I; why no replied he nor I neither: – I speak Madam only of *vulgar Souls*: and yet I think Spirits are the Things I am generally most in Dread of: but said I you are not much in dread of them methinks; for you lye without a Light in your Room, and you are for ever walking about both House & Gardens in the Dark – as if on purpose to encounter them. To be sure my Dearest replies Mr Johnson I am not afraid of Spirits *at all*; yet I think if I was to be afraid of anything it *would be* of Spirits.*

Now all this put me in Mind of what Beauclerck said at Brighthelmstone, that Johnson was afraid of Spirits; and I suppose he has in some humour professed as much; and then, the good humour'd kind Friends he has – explain this *no Fear* of his into Guilt, Cowardice and I know not what; like his telling People in another Whim that he don't know Greek – whereas there is no Wit in setting the World against one more than it is; & if it is foolish to say things in *Praise* of one's Self, 'tis foolisher to say Things in *Dis*praise, even when strictly true, which is really not the Case here, either respecting the Ghosts or the Greek.

All This Stuff ✎ He used another Expression too sometimes that fretted me: when People abused him in the publick Prints I have heard him say – well! if the Dogs knew me now but half as well as I know myself, they might say Things that *would* vex me; but all *this Stuff* why – what care I for't? now *I* who knew perfectly what that *was* had a mortal Aversion to this Talk.*

Abuse ✎ Every body knows how little Mr Johnson valued Abuse, Aquila says he non capit Muscas;* and he thought that therefore no exalted Character had need to mind it – they teize one says he, but as a Fly stings a horse.

He was however very much nettled by Churchill's Satire* that's certain; for he rejected him from among the Poets when the Booksellers begged him a Place in the Edition they are now giving in small Volumes – this was I think the only unjust or resentful Thing I ever knew him do, for as to despising Churchill as a Writer – no Man has Pretensions to do it – and Johnson had more Wit to be sure than not to taste the *Prophecy of Famine*.

The True Christian ✎ Johnson has been often in the Course of these wretched Gleanings compared to Rousseau; he resembled him however in two Things more important than any

I have mentioned yet – his Fear of Death, & his high Notions of the hard Task of Christianity – He never thinks that he has done or can do enough, – and dreads the Time when he shall be beaten with many Stripes – Le vrai Chretien says Jean Jacques – in the same Spirit – trouve tous Jours son Tâche audessus de soi;* the whole passage is beautiful but I have not it by me, & quite on Johnson's Principle. – I shewed it him once and he said so too.

Death Glutted ∽ Seeing the Death of one Sam: Johnson in the Paper last Week, & in a few Days another of the same Name; – why all this will make you low spirited said I; on the contrary returned the Doctor; Death has I hope been glutted with Sam: Johnsons, he has had so many of late, and he will now spare me for some Time to come.

A Catalogue of Writings ∽ Here will I give a Catalogue of such Writings as I *know* to be his, there are many that *I do not know* – scattered about the World.

Dictionary–	Life of Blake, Drake, & the K: of Prussia.
Debates in Parl^t Pitts 1st Speech	
Rambler.	False Alarm, Falklands Islands – & Taxation no Tyranny.
Confutation of Soame Jennings.	
Idler.–	Patriot
Observations on Tea in the Lit^y Magazine	Dedication to Payne's Book of Draughts.
Papers sign'd T. in the Adventurer, sent thither under the Notion of their being written by Dr Bathurst.	Dedication to Percys Ballads.
	Dedication to Burney on Musick.
	Dedication to Adams on the Globes.
Preface & Notes to Shakespeare.	Travels of Father Lobo – his 1st Work.
Preface to the World Displayed.	
Preface to Rolts Dict: of Commerce	Life of Brown, Savage, & Barrettiere.
Rasselas.	Hermit of Teneriffe.

[67]

Project for an Infirmary at Hereford.
Sermons for Strahan & Hervey – I know not how many.
Law Lectures for Chambers.
some things in the Visitor.
The Tale of Floretta or the three Fountains in Miss Williams's Miscellanies.
Letters in the Gazetteer about Black Fryars Bridge–
Plan for the Coronation.
Irene–
Prologue to the opening of the Theatre.

D⁰ to the Goodnatured Man,
d⁰ for Kelly's Widow,
D⁰ for Milton's Granddaughter.
Vanity of human Wishes.
London.
Busy curious Thirsty Fly made Latin wch Langton has, & some Latin Verses to Dr Lawrence. & a Copy of Verses in Dodsley which he never would tell me, though he trusted me with Secrets of far greater Importance.

Johnson's Character ∽ One Evening as I was giving my Tongue Liberty to praise Mr Johnson to his Face; a favour he would not often allow me he said in high good humour; come! you shall draw up my Character your own Way, & shew it me; that I may see what you will say of me when I am gone. at Night I wrote as follows –

His Appearance ∽ It is usual – I know not why, when a Character is given, to begin with a Description of the Person: – that which contained the Soul of Mr Johnson, deserves to be particularly described. His Stature was remarkably high, and his Limbs exceedingly large; his Strength was more than common I believe, & his Activity was greater than his Size gave one Cause to expect. his Features were strongly marked, though his Complexion was fair, a Circumstance somewhat unusual: his Sight was near, and otherwise imperfect, yet his Eyes though of a light blue Colour were so wild, so piercing, and at Times so fierce; that Fear was I believe the first Emotion in the hearts of all his Beholders.

[68]

His Mind ↬ His Mind was so Comprehensive that no Language but his own could have express'd its Contents, & so ponderous was his Language that Sentiments less lofty & less solid than his was; would have been encumbered, not adorned by it: – Mr Johnson was however no pompous Converser, & though he was accused of using big Words, it was only when little ones would not express his meaning as clearly, or when the Elevation of the thought would have been disgraced by a Dress less superb.

His Mirth ↬ He used to say that the size of a mans Understanding might always be known by his Mirth, and his own was never contemptible: he would laugh at a Stroke of Absurdity, or a Saillie of genuine Humour more heartily than I almost ever saw a man, and though the Jest was often such as few felt besides himself, yet his Laugh was irresistible, & was observed immediately to produce that of the Company, not merely from the notion that it was proper to laugh when he did, but purely for want of Power to forbear it.

Life's Trappings ↬ He was no Enemy to Splendour of Apparel, or Pomp of Equipage; Life he would say sometimes is but too barren with all her Trappings, let us therefore be cautious how we strip her.

His Soul ↬ Mr Johnson had indeed when I knew him first looked on Life till he was weary; for as a Mind slow in its own nature, or unenlivened by Information will contentedly read in the same Book for twenty Times perhaps; the very Effort of reading it, being more than half the Business; & every Period being at every Reading better understood; while a Mind more active or more skilful to comprehend its meaning is made sincerely sick at the second Perusal: so a Soul like his, acute to discern the Truth, vigorous to embrace, and powerful to retain it, soon sees enough of the World's dull Prospect, which at first like that of the Sea pleases by its Extent, but soon like that too fatigues from its Uniformity: a Calm and a Storm being the only Variations which the Nature of either will admit of.

Like A Cube ∽ Of Mr Johnson's Learning the World has been the Judge, and were I to produce a score of his sayings as a Proof of his Wit, it would be like shewing a handful of Oriental Pearl to evince the Riches of the great Mogul. Suffice it at once that he was great on all Occasions, and like a Cube in Architecture you beheld him on each Side, & his Size still appeared undiminished.

His Heart ∽ The heart of this Man was however not a hard one; but susceptible of Gratitude, & of every kind impression: yet tho' he had refined his Sensibility he had not endangered his Quiet by encouraging in himself a Solicitude about Trifles, which he treated with the neglect they Deserve.

His Roughness ∽ It is well known that Mr Johnson had a roughness in his Manner which subdued the saucy & terrified the Meek; this was when I knew him the prominent Part of a Character which few durst venture to approach so nearly, & which was for that Reason in many Respects – so grossly, and so frequently mistaken, & it was perhaps peculiar to him, that the noble Consciousness of Superiority which animated his Looks, and raised his Voice in Conversation; cast likewise an impenetrable Veil over him when he said nothing, his Talk had therefore commonly the Complexion of Arrogance, his Silence of Superciliousness.

Seldom Silent ∽ He was however seldom inclined to be silent when any Moral or Literary Subject was proposed, & it was on such Occasions that like the Sage in Rasselas he spoke & Attention watched his Lips; he reason'd and Conviction closed his periods. if Poetry was talked of, his Quotations were the readiest; & had he not been eminent for more solid & brilliant Qualities, Mankind would have united to extol his extraordinary Memory. his manner of repeating too deserves to be described tho' at the same [time] it defeats all Power of Description.

His Veracity ↶ His Equity in giving the Character of another ought not undoubtedly to be omitted in his own, whence Partiality and Prejudice were totally excluded; a Steadiness of Conduct the more to be commended, as no Man had stronger Likings or Aversions. His Veracity was indeed on all occasions strict even to severity; he scorned to embellish a Story with fictitious Circumstances which he used to say took off from its real Value; a Story says Johnson "" "should be a Specimen of Life and Manners; but if the surrounding Circumstances are false, as it is no longer any Representation of Reality it is no longer worthy our Attention"" ".

For ever Revered ↶ For the rest; that Beneficence which during his Life increased the Comforts of so many, may after his Death be ungratefully forgotten; but that Piety which dictated the serious Papers in the Rambler will be for ever remembred, for ever I think – revered. That ample Repository of religious Truth, moral Wisdom & accurate Criticism breathes indeed the genuine Emanations of its Author's Mind; express'd too in a Style so natural to him, & So much like his common Mode of conversing, that I was myself not much astonished when he told me, that he had scarcely read over one of those inimitable Essays before they were sent to the Press.

One Peculiarity ↝ I will add one peculiarity before I finish his Character: Tho' a man of obscure Birth, His partiality to People of Family was visible on every Occasion: his Zeal for Subordination warm even to Bigotry, his hatred for Innovation & Reverence for the old feudal Times, apparent whenever any possible means of shewing them occurred.

Blemishes ↝ I have spoken of his Piety, his Charity & his Truth; the Enlargement of his Heart, & the Delicacy of his Sentiments: & when I search for the Blemishes in a Character so compleat none will present itself to my Sight, but Pride modified differently, as different Opportunities shewed it in different Forms; yet his Pride was ever nicely purified at once from meanness and from Vanity –

A Royal Pleasure Ground ↝ The mind of Mr Johnson was indeed expanded beyond the common Limits of human Nature, & stored with such variety of Knowledge that I used to think it resembled a Royal Pleasure Ground, where every Tree of every Name & Nation, flourished in the full perfection of their Nature; & where tho' lofty Woods & falling Cataracts first caught the Eye, & fixed the Attention of Beholders, yet neither the trim Parterre, nor the pleasing Shrubbery; nor even the antiquated Evergreens were denied a Place in some fit Corner of the happy Valley.

A Very Fine Piece of Writing ↝ When I shewed him his Character next day – for he would see it; he said it was a very fine Piece of Writing; and that I had improved upon *Young* who he saw was my *Model* he said; for my Flattery was still stronger than *his*, & yet somehow or other less *hyperbolical*.

Harris's Dedication ↝ Of James Harris Dedication to his Hermes he said that tho' but 14 Lines long, there were 6

Grammatical faults in it.

Elphinstone's Martial ∽ Of Elphinstone's specimen of Martial he said, there was too much Folly in them for Madness, and too much Madness for Folly.

Mrs Thrale's Martial ∽ I had in some humour in the Year 1768 imitated one of Martial's Epigrams myself in the Character of
Doctor Johnson
here it is

> Swelling with Envy see some Wretch appears,
> While hourly quoted Ramblers grieve his Ears;
> Swelling with Envy eyes the crowded Park,
> Where Shrugs significant my Person mark;
> Swelling with Envy sees one Pension paid
> To conscious Worth that scorns the flattring Trade;
> Swelling with Envy sees the calm Retreat
> That Streatham's Shades afford my weary Feet,
> Swelling with Envy hears the meaner Fame
> That Johnson's Court to Johnson owes its Name;†
> Swelling with Envy sees each Friend I love
> Pleas'd while corrected, & while check'd – approve:
> Swelling with Envy which affords no Pow'r
> To damp the Pleasures of my social Hour
> See him with Envy swelled, and Spleen accurst,
> But if he *swells* with Envy – let him *burst*.

Abuse of Warton ∽ When Tom Warton published his Poems in Jan: 1777. – nobody read 'em – Warton's Poems are *come out* says Mr Johnson; yes replied I, & this cold Weather has *struck them in* again: I have written Verses to abuse them says he, but I can repeat but two or three of them, & those you

† He lodged in Johnson's Court – so called I believe because he lodged in it.

must say nothing of, for I love Thomas look you – tho' I laugh at him.†

here they are.

> Wheresoe'er I turn my View,
> All is strange, yet nothing new;
> Endless Labour all along,
> Endless Labour to be wrong;
> Phrase that Time has flung away,
> Uncouth Words in Disarray:
> Trickt in Antique Ruff and Bonnet,
> Ode and Elegy and Sonnet.

Improvisation ∾ Baretti and I were talking one Day of the Art of Improvisation: Johnson says he, can do it as well as any Italian of us all if he pleases; I once repeated him these Lines of an Improvisatore spoken when the Duke of Modena ran away for Fear of the Comet

> Se al venir vostro i Principi sen' vanno,
> Deh venga ogni Di, – durate un Anno. –

which he instantly rendered thus–

> If at your coming – Princes disappear,
> Comets come every day – and stay a Year.

These foolish French Verses too – in a Pantomime.

† Long after this, he, in Scorn of the same Author Tom Warton, composed extempore the following comical Lines.

1.

> Hermit hoar in solemn Cell
>   Wearing out Life's Evening grey,
> Strike thy Bosom Sage and tell
>   Where is Bliss & which the way.

2.

> Thus I spoke, and speaking sigh'd
>   Scarce repress'd the starting Tear;
> When the hoary Sage replied
>   Come my Lad, and drink some Beer.

These Verses have of late run about the Town – I gave them Pepys and he has shew'd off with them for a whole Winter.

[74]

> Je suis Cassandre descendu des Cieux
> Pour vous faire entendre – Mesdames et Messieurs,
> Que Je suis Cassandre deçendu des Cieux. –

which he translated thus – Improviso.

> I am Cassander, come down from the Sky,
> To tell each Bystander – what none can deny
> That I am Cassander come down from the Sky.

Another Instance ∽ Another more humourous Instance of his Powers of Improvisation. I was praising these Verses of Lope de Vega.

> Si a quien los Leones vence,
> Vence una Muger hermosa;
> El de mas flaco s'averguence
> O ella de ser mas furiosa.*

they are well enough replied Johnson, but the Conceit is not clear: the Lady as we all know does not conquer as the Lyon does – 'tis merely a Play of Words as if I should say

> If the Man who Turneps cries
> Cry not when his Father dies;
> 'Tis a Sign that he had rather
> Have a Turnep than a Father.

A Reply to Sheridan ∽ This is of the same Species of Humour as his reply to Sheridan who was commending with ridiculous Vehemence the following Line

> Who rules oer Freemen should himself be free:

to be sure Sir replied Johnson hastily and

> Who drives fat Oxen should himself be fat.

Translation of Baretti ∽ He likewise translated those Pretty Italian Lines of Mr Baretti at the End of the small Talk very elegantly and all in a Minute

Viva Viva la Padrona!
Tutta bella e tutta buona;
La Padrona un Angiolella
Tutta buona & tutta bella,
Tutta bella & tutta buona
Viva Viva la Padrona! –

Long may live my lovely Hetty!
Always Young and always pretty;
Always pretty, always Young,
Live my lovely Hetty long;
Always Young & always pretty
Long may live my lovely Hetty!

On Being Thirty Five ◊ And this Year 1777 when I told him it was my Birthday & that I was then thirty five Years old – He repeated me these Verses which I wrote down from his Mouth as he made them.

Oft in Danger yet alive
We are come to Thirty five;
Oft may better Years arrive,
Better Years than thirty five:
Could Philosophers contrive,
Life to stop at Thirty five,
Time his hours should never drive
O'er the bounds of Thirty five:
High to soar and deep to dive
Nature gives at Thirty five:
Ladies – stock and tend your Hive,
Trifle not at Thirty five!
For howeer we boast and strive
Life declines from Thirty five;
He that ever hopes to thrive
Must begin by Thirty five;
And those who wisely wish to wive
Must look on *Thrale* at Thirty five. –

Translation of Metastasio ◊ This Italian Song too of Metastasio as Baretti and I were commending it – he turned into English instantly

> Deh! se piacermi vuoi
> Lascia i Sospetti tuoi,
> Non mi turbar con questa
> Molesta dubitar:
>
> Chi ciecamente crede
> Impegna a serbar Fede;
> Chi sempre Inganno aspetta,
> Alletta ad Ingannar.

   as Thus –

> Would you hope to gain my heart,
> Bid your teizing Doubts depart;
> He who blindly trusts will find
> Faith from ev'ry generous Mind,
> He who still expects Deceit,
> Only teaches how to cheat.†

Another Translation ∽ Another favourite Passage too in the same Author; which Baretti made his Pupil – my eldest Daughter get by heart – Johnson translated into Blank Verse – *sur le Champ*: Baretti wrote it down from his Lips, and I write it now from Baretti's Copy, which is almost worne out with lying by in the folds.

> Parlata D'Emirena al falso Cortigiano Aquilio –
>
> Ah! tu in Corte invecchiasti, e giurerei
> Che fra i pochi non sei tenace ancora

---

† Likewise the famous *Rio Verde* of the Spanish Poet which he render'd Impromptu thus

> Glassy Water, Glassy Water
> Down whose Current clear & strong
> Chiefs confus'd in mutual Slaughter
> Moor and Christian roll along.

perhaps this is mention'd elsewhere.

[77]

> Dell' antica Onestà! Quando bisogna
> Saprai, sereno in Volto
> Vezzeggiare un Nemico. Acciò vi cadá
> Aprirgli innanzi un Precipizio; e poi
> Piangerne la Caduta. Offrirti a tutti
> E non esser che tuo: Di false Lodi
> Vestir le Accuse, ed aggravar le Colpe
> Nel farne la difesa – Ognor dal Trono
> I buoni allontanar – D'ogni castigo
> Lasciar l'odio allo Scettro & d'ogni dono
> Il Merito usurpar: tener nascosto
> Sotto un Zelo apparente un empio fine
> Ne fabbricar che sulle altrui Rovine.

Emirena's Speech in the Opera of Adriano by Metastastio.

> Grown old in Courts, thou art not surely one
> That keeps the rigid Rules of ancient Honor;
> Well skill'd to sooth a foe with Looks of Kindness,
> To sink the fatal Precipice before them
> And then lament their Fall with seeming Friendship,
> Open to all, true only to thyself,
> Thou knowst those Arts which blast with envious Praise
> Which aggravate a Fault with feign'd Excuse,
> And drive discountenanc'd Virtue from the Throng.
> That leave the blame of Rigour to the Prince,
> And yet of every Gift usurp the Merit;
> That hide in seeming Zeal a wicked purpose
> And only build upon another's Ruin –

A Temple to the Winds ∽ The Verses too which – with the true Gratitude of a Wit – Johnson made at my Lord Anson's,* – when the Owner with great Politeness walked over the Grounds with him, & shewed him among other Things – **a Temple to the Winds** – were done Improviso and are pretty enough

> Gratum Animum laudo; qui debuit omnia *Ventis*
> Quam bene ventorum, surgere *Templa* jubet.*

[78]

Dryden's Epigram ↶ The following famous Epigram of Dryden's likewise is elegantly Latinized in the six following Lines.

> Quos laudet Vates, Graius, Romanus et Anglus,
> Tres tria temporibus Secla dedere suis:
> Sublime Ingenium Graius, Romanus habebat
> Carmen grande sonans; Anglus utrumque tulit
> Nil majus Natura capit clarare priores,
> Quæ potuere duos, tertius unus habet.*

Benserade's Verses ↶ And when somebody was praising Benserade's Verses a son Lit

> Theatre des Ris et des Pleurs,
> Lit ou je nais et ou je meurs;
> Tu nous fais voir comment Voisins,
> Sont nos Plaisirs et nos Chagrins.

he instantly cry'd out–

> In Bed we laugh, in Bed we cry,
> And born in Bed – in Bed we dye,
> The near Approach a Bed may shew
> Of human Bliss to human Woe.

Mr Banks's Goat ↶ The Inscription upon Mr Banks's Goat's Collar too is exquisite – She had been on two of his Adventurous Expeditions* with him, and he at last hired or bought a Field for her somewhere in Kent, where She was to graze in Peace for the remainder of her Life – he put her on a Collar however, & these two Lines were written round it by Mr Johnson at Banks's Request.

> Perpetui ambita bis Terra, premia lactis
> Hæc habet altrici Capra, seconda Jovis. *

Johnson at the Oratorio ↶ One Night in Feb: 1771. or later in the Spring – Oratorio Season I made Mr Johnson go with me to one we sate in a Side Box. he soon however left off listening to the Musick but said little, so I thought he was minding it: when we came home however he repeated me the following Verses which he had been composing at the Play house it seems.

In Theatro.

Tertii verso quater orbe lustri
Quid theatrales tibi Crispe pompæ!
Quam decet Canos male literatos
     Sera Voluptas.

Tene mulceri fidibus canoris?
Tene cantorum modulis stupere?
Tene per pictas oculo Elegante
     Currere formas?

Inter æquales sine felle liber,
Codices, veri studiosus inter
Rectius vives, sua quisque carpat
     Gaudia gratus.

Lusibus gaudet puer otiosis
Luxus oblectat Iuvenem theatri
At seni fluxo sapienter uti
     Tempore restat.

Mrs Thrale's Translation ~ I took it into my Head I could imitate these Verses, so I tried the next Morning, & shewed Mr Johnson my Performance: – he rather commended all but the last Stanza – which he said was too wide from the Original.

Here they are.

When Threescore Years have chang'd thee quite
Still can Theatric Scenes delight?
Ill suits this Place with learned Wight
   May Bates or Coulson† cry.

† two of his old College Companions at Oxford.

> The Scholar's Pride can Brent disarm?
> His Heart can soft Guadagni warm?*
> Or Scenes with sweet delusion charm
> > The Climacterick Eye?
>
> The social Club, the lonely Tower,†
> Far better suit thy Midnight hour,
> Let each according to his Power
> > In Worth or Wisdom shine!
>
> And whilst Play pleases idle Boys,
> And wanton Mirth fond Youth employs,
> To fix the Mind – and free from Toys
> > That useful Task be thine.

A Sad Man in a Publick Place ∽ Johnson was however a sad Man to carry to a publick Place, for every body knew him, & he drew all Eyes upon one; & by his odd Gestures & perhaps loud Voice got People to stare at one in a very disagreable Manner.

An Ode from Skie ∽ With his Ode written in the Isle of Skie and addressed to *Me* I shall close – for the present at least – my Account of Mr Johnson – it has taken up near a hundred Pages I see.

> Permeo terras, ubi nuda rupes
> Saxeas miscet nebulis ruinas,
> Torva ubi rident steriles coloni
> > Rura labores.
>
> Pervagor Gentes, hominum ferorum
> Vita ubi nullo decorata cultu
> Squallet informis, tugurique fumis
> > Fœda latescit.

† we used to call his Room at our House – the round Tower.

> Inter Errores, salebrosa longi
> Inter ignotæ strepitus loquelæ
> Quot modis mecum, quid agat requiro,
> **Thralia** dulcis.
>
> Seu Viri cures, pia nupta mulcet,
> Seu fovet mater sobolem benigna
> Sive cum Libris novitate pascit
> Sedula mentem:
>
> Sit memor nostri fideique merces,
> Stet fides constans, meritoque blandum
> **Thraliæ** discant resonare Nomen
> Littora Skiae.*
> Scriptum in Skia Sept: 6: 1773.

An Old Man's Child ↝ An Old man's Child says Johnson leads much the same sort of Life as a Child's Dog; teized like that with Fondness through Folly, and exhibited like that to every Company, through idle and empty Vanity.

Education like Agriculture ↝ I have heard Johnson observe that as Education is often compared to Agriculture, so it resembles it chiefly in this; that though no one can tell whether the Crop may answer the Culture, yet if nothing be sowed, we all see that no Crop can be obtained.

Warburton ↝ Johnson once observed of Warburton* in my hearing, that he was like a man who goes to War so much overloaden with Armour that he never has it in his power to fight.

Foote ↝ Johnson & Bodens* were talking here one Day of Foote,* & I was in haste to write down the Conversation; after mentioning many of his peculiarities – Foote (says Mr Johnson) is particularly clever at an Escape; that Fellow is never wholly subdued by any Argument, & I have sometimes fancied him like a Man who when one has driven him up into a Corner & held him in with an arm on each side he suddenly gives a Spring and leaps over your head – or says the Colonel rather like a Duck, who seems just devoted to the Jaws of the dog, then dipping on a sudden in the Water, you see her five Minutes after feathering herself at the further end of the Canal.

Compared to Garrick ∽ Foote and Garrick were next compar'd as Mimicks, they have a different walk says Johnson & are as distinct in their powers of Mimickry, as Swift and Addison in their powers of humour. Swift could draw a prominent Character, & Foote can imitate to equal perfection the Tricks & Contorsions of some particular Man: Foote for Example can personate Langford, he can not exhibit the general Idea of an Auctioneer. Foote can not act a Miser, but he can transcribe the Actions Face & Language of some well known close-fisted Citizen. Thus Addison remains unrivalled in the power of Ridicule when a Character was to be made whom every Person will be struck with as having seen somebody that it will fit, while the Dean can but render ridiculous a certain Character by the less valuable arts of Caricatura.

Colonel Bodens's Conversation ∽ Of Colonel Bodens's Conversation I once heard Johnson say that it reminded him of the Aloe Tree; that blossoms once in a hundred Years, & whose Shoot is attended with a cracking Noise resembling an Explosion; when that is over all is quiet till the return of the periodical Effort.

Her Mother's Epitaph ∽ Epitaph on Hester Maria Salusbury by Dr Samuel Johnson

Juxta sepulta est Hestera Maria,
Thomæ Cotton de Combermere Baroneti Cestriensis Filia,
Joanni Salusbury Armigeri Flintiensis, Uxor;
Forma felix, felix Ingenio,
Omnibus jucunda, suorum amantissima,
Linguis Artibusque ita exculta
Ut Colloquijs nunquam deessent
Sermonis nitor, sententiarum flosculi,
Sapientiæ gravitas, leporum gratia;
Modum servandi adeo perita
ut domestica inter negotia literis oblectaretur,
Literarum inter delicias rem familiarem sedulo curaret
Multis illi, multos annos precantibus
 Cancri insanabilis venemo contabuit,
Nexibusque vitæ paulatim resolutis,
 Terris – meliora sperans – emigravit. –
Nata 1706. Nupta 1739. Obiit – 1773. *

Epitaph on a Dog ∽ With regard to little French Epitaphs I have always had an Itch to translate them, & some times have fancied that I could do them successfully; here is one written I know not by whom on a Dog.

> Aboyant les Larrons sans cesse,
> Muet a l'Amant favori;
> J'ay etè egalement cheri
> De mon Maitre et de ma Maitresse.

Render'd thus.

> With my Lord nor my Lady I ne'er had Dispute,
> For at Robbers I bark'd and to Lovers was mute.

This however is I find not Original in the French, here is an Italian one on the same Subject.

> Agli Ladron' ladrai, ed a gl'Amanti tacqui,
> Cosi ed a Messer, ed a Madonna piacqui.

Oh Heavens! here is one in Latin too; That I suppose was first written of them all.

> Latratu fures excepi, mutus Amantes,
> Sic placui Domino, sic placui Dominæ.

Johnson translates it thus

> To Robbers furious, and to Lovers tame,
> I pleas'd my Master, and I pleas'd my Dame.*

Parental Affection ∽ Doctor Collier* used to say speaking of Parental Affection that one loved one's Children in Anticipation, one hopes they will one day become useful, estimable, & amiable Beings – one cannot love lumps of Flesh continued he, and they are nothing better during Infancy.

On the same Subject I have heard Johnson say one can hardly help wishing while one fondles a Baby, that it never would grow up to Man's Estate; but remain always an innocent & amiable Creature, when it becomes a Man, 'tis a Thousand to one but one shall either detest or despise it.

Counting One's Money ∽ Doctor Collier used to say that one might discern Generosity or Avarice merely by observing the manner of a Man who was counting out his Money; it sticks says he even literally to the Fingers of a Fellow truly covetous. Now says Mr Johnson when I told this to him, here is neither Virtue nor Vice concerned, but the use alone or disuse of counting out Money – Let a Gentleman for example of 3000£ a Year Landed Estate lose 500£ by a Tenant he will talk on't for ever till he wearies His Friends his Children & his Neighbours. Let a Man on the other hand who gains 3000£ a Year by a prosperous Trade lose 500£ by a bad Debt – he shall not even mention it – no nor *think* of it out of his Counting house. the Secret is – that the Trader is familiar with the Sight of 500£ & of ten Times as much; but the Landed Gentleman who never sees his Gold in heaps, never gets acquainted with it; nor can bear the Thoughts of parting, when it is so unlikely they should meet again.

An Angel's Imprimatur ~ Addison wrote with the greatest Scrupulosity for fear of doing harm of any Man before Johnson; but as Mrs Montagu* says if an Angel was to give an Imprimatur, he would give it to none but Johnson.

Shaftsbury Chubb ~ I have heard Mr Johnson say myself that he never would give Shaftsbury Chubb* or any wicked Writer's Authority for a Word, lest it should send People to look in a Book that might injure them for ever.

James Harris ~ One said James Harris* was a learned Man; for ought I know replied Johnson, but Learning should not be trusted in such hands – tis giving a Sword to a Man that is paralytick.

A Foolish Fellow ~ Is not young Rose Fuller* a foolish Fellow said I to keep from Church because old Rose is an Infidel? – Is it not foolisher says Johnson in James Harris to be an Infidel, because Lord Shaftsbury wrote the Characteristicks?

An Odd Book ~ Here is an odd Book* come out to prove Falstaff was no Coward, when says Johnson will one come forth to prove Iago an honest Man?

What is Circumcision? ~ Mr Johnson told me that at a Friends house he had been one Evening talking over some Theological Subjects – the Room was full – a Young Lady said to him: Now pray dear Sir tell us what was that Circumcision we so read of – Ask your Mama tomorrow Miss said he.†

---

† Pray What is the Difference between a Bull & an Ox? says a little Boy to his Tutress; the Bull is the Calf's Papa my Dear replies She, & the Ox is his Uncle. I can't think why, but this is very comical.

Mrs Jackson ↝ Mrs Jackson* – the daughter of old Martin the optician was a Woman of very uncommon Accomplishments; skilled in Astronomy Painting and Musick – some of her Drawings are really excellent, and for Geography, I have known no Person who had so thorough a Knowledge of it: but no more common Sense had She than a Baby, which Johnson attributed to her having spent her Youth in acquiring Embellishments which were useless, instead of a solid Understanding – Such Tricks says he have no Power at all to advance Intellect, they neither grow out of a Character nor sink into one, they are apparently stuck on the Surface: Such Accomplishments says he on another occasion, but speaking I think of the same Woman, – are like Spangles, they catch the Attention & fix it on the Trimming, but if the Lace be not rich The Spangles were better away; they serve only to shew that the whole is frippery.

The Finery of a Beggar ↝ Johnson loves somewhat *solid* in every thing better than somewhat shining – I shew'd Him a gay Satten one day it was very showy tho' slight, poor Mrs Jackson wore it: Is not this *fine* said I? Yes reply'd he – *'tis the finery of a Beggar.*

Et in Arcadia Ego ↝ I was much surprized when Johnson related to me the following Fact: he had been at Club over night, and there was Talk of Sir Joshua's Portrait of the two famous beautiful Friends Mrs Bouverie and Mrs Crewe: he had drawn them in a pleasing Landscape, and pensive Attitudes with the well known Motto Et in Arcadia ego. at the Bottom of the Picture. Says Mr Johnson what is to be understood by that Motto I beg to know – it does not seem to convey any particular Meaning: – Not a soul in that wise Club could tell – one said it meant nothing but an Arcadian Scene, and that the Beholder looking on was supposed to

VII SIR JOSHUA REYNOLDS
*Engraved by T. W. Hunt,
after a painting by Sir Joshua Reynolds,
The National Portrait Gallery, London*

cry out – *Now I am in Arcadia*! & such Stuff: but in short none of them knew that the Thought was borrowed from N: Poussin who places three Shepherds & a Nymph or two in a showy Landschape with a *Tomb* in the Back Ground and a Death's Head on it with this Motto – *Et in Arcadia Ego* – *Mors loquitur* of Course: Mr Johnson who despised Connoisseurship exceedingly, might reasonably have been suspected of Ignorance on such a Subject – but Reynolds himself to borrow the Motto, when he understood not the meaning – Oh Fye!*

Sir Joshua ∽ Johnson once said speaking of Sir Joshua Reynolds – there goes a Man not to be spoiled by Prosperity.

Mr Fitzherbert ∽ It was on the 10th Day of August 1770. that I saw Mr Fitzherbert* for the first Time, he pleased me mighty well but I expected more Wit, more Flash than I found in him; Johnson says that it is by having *no* Wit, & pretending to none that he has gained such considerable Ground upon the World, that 'tis now half a Disgrace not to be acquainted with Fitzherbert: he added a peculiarity of Character which doubtless contributes to forward his *Reputation* – *Reception* I mean; & that is, that no Man is less welcome to Fitzherbert either for his Virtues or for his Vices; he is as willing says Johnson to shew Friendship to Sam: Johnson as to Dick Swift† – to *Rousseau* as to *Saint Austin.*

A Bon Mot ∽ Fitzherbert related a Bon Mot of Johnson's one Day when I met him at Nesbitt's Dinner; – *any* Man may relate another's Wit said Pottinger, let's have some of your own pray: you are mistaken sir replies Fitzherbert, it is not every Man that *can* relate a Bon Mot, and Tom Davies spoyl'd this very one last Week – I heard him.

† Dick Swift was a famous Robber about that time.

Painted by Sir Joshua Reynolds.   *Engraved by E. Finden.*

James Boswell

VIII JAMES BOSWELL

This was the Bon Mot – that is if I can tell it – Boswell had long wished to get acquainted with Johnson, & had press'd Davies to introduce him, but Davies durst not: meeting him however accidentally in the Shop, Boswell resolved to introduce himself – and coming towards him said *modestly* Sir I have long wished for the honour of conversing with so great a Man, but have always been apprehensive You would not like me because I was a Scotsman, now I *could* not *help coming out* of Scotland – you know: No Sir replies Johnson I see none of you that *can*.

Poor Davies it seems told the Story thus; I could not you know help being a *Scotsman*, no Sir says Johnson I see none of you that *can* – This was spoyling the Bon Mot indeed.

On the 3^d of January this famous Fitzherbert hanged himself, leaving Mankind much astonished at his conduct: And now says Johnson see what it is to have a diffus'd Acquaintance and not one Friend.

Sir Joshua Reynolds ∽ Sir Joshua is indeed sufficiently puffed up with the Credit he has acquired for his written Discourses, a Praise he is more pleased with than that he obtains by his Profession; besides that he seems to set up as a Sort of Patron to Literature; so that no Book goes rapidly thro' a first Edition now, but the Author is at Reynolds's Table in a Trice: Mr Johnson, who is naturally disposed to find every thing *right* in the moral World from a Perswasion that it cannot be much better I believe – says that Sir Joshua came into his fortune too late to arrive at general Knowledge by the regular Progress of Study – and so says he he calls the World about him, and catches with Avidity at all Literary Conversation. Of late however since he has found his Friend delight in the Company of Infidels he rather thinks somethings wrong I believe, but Sir Joshua is now quite above caring what he thinks of the matter.

Animal Substances ∽ Mr Johnson once made me observe that none but Animal Substances were ever said to be nasty.

Oliver Goldsmith ∽ Graham of Eton* had spent the Afternoon in Company with Johnson & Goldsmith;* they had been very agreable I suppose, so when Graham was got warm with Wine and Kindness – Sir says he I should be vastly happy to see you at Eton, where I would shew you every Civility in my Power. Sir, replies Goldsmith I am extremely obliged to you. – Nay *Doctor Minor* cries the other – dont think I mean *you*. Very fine indeed grumbles Goldsmith, now this is a fellow to make one commit *Suicide*.

Nobody Makes a Bustle ∽ One Day when Murphy and many more Wits were called to a Dinner at Davies's – Tom Davies – who swears by Johnson – was rejoycing to hear he was come safe to Town – from Lincolnshire I think – he had been a Summer at Langton's – Ay Ay – come set your Bells a ringing do says Goldsmith –what can be the Reason though that nobody makes a Bustle when *I* come in or out of Town.

Little Goldee ∽ It being observed that Dr Goldsmith was greatly disconcerted by a smart Repartie, so much indeed that he would forbear to attack if he at all expected Defence; True interrupted Johnson our little Goldee would like best to be witty on a deaf Man.

Goodman Dull ∽ Somebody had abused Johnson & Goldsmith in the papers – calling them by the names of the Pedant & Constable in Love's Labour lost: Goldsmith was in the utmost perplexity – ready to cry: – what Folly says his Friend to be vexed thus about nothing. – what *harm* can it do a Man to call him Holofernes? it may do you no harm to be called *Holofernes*, replies the other – but I don't like to be *Goodman Dull*.

IX OLIVER GOLDSMITH
*Engraved by G. Marchi,
after a painting by Sir Joshua Reynolds,
The National Portrait Gallery, London*

In Westminster Abbey ↶ The two Doctors were roving together about the Town in an idle humour, and having strolled into Westminster Abbey as they walked through the Poets Corner – Mr Johnson turned to his Companion and said

Forsitan et Nomen nostrum miscebitur illis.*

they proceeded in their Walk, and having called on a Friend that way, were led to pass Temple Bar, when Goldsmith recollecting their Jacobitism & looking up to the Traytor's Heads said to Mr Johnson

Forsitan et Nomen nostrum miscebitur *illis**

this was the best thing I ever heard of Goldsmith's Conversation Wit.

At the Chaplain's Table ↶ One Sunday that He & Mr Johnson dined at the Chaplain's Table; some body quoted this Line from Virgil

Premit altum Corde dolorem.*

Ay says Doctor Goldsmith I know how that is by experience; for when my Play was hissed two Years ago, I looked as merry as I do now, and went to the Club at night, and laughed and sung I remember the Song of the Old Woman toss'd in a Blanket, and yet says he, – (the Parsons began to stare:) – and yet says he, when all the Company was retired except Mr Johnson & myself, I fairly burst *out o' crying* with Vexation. – So you did indeed Doctor says Johnson; but I thought till now it had been a secret, I am sure I would not have told it for the World.

Goldsmith & the Chest ↶ Goldsmith's Curiosity was as drôle as his Vanity: he saw a great Cedar Chest in my House once & nothing would serve him but know what was within: I was from home it seems – his Visit was to Johnson. what makes you so uneasy says Mr Johnson – why says he I long to pick the Lock of that Chest so – do dear Mr Johnson look if none of your Keys will undo it – when I came home & heard this Folly, I opened the Chest immediately & shewed him it was empty – Marplot* does nothing more ridiculous upon the Stage.

Goldsmith's Ill Will ○ The real ill Will he manifestly bore to every equal, & every Superior made him hateful; he actually seemed to rejoyce in Johnson's temporary Depression from Illness, and whispered Mr Thrale who never loved him afterwards – that Johnson would never more be the Man he was. This was bad indeed when one considers that it was Mr Johnson who first drew him out of Obscurity, and set him upon a heighth that made him giddy. His ill Will however was not confined to those he was obliged to – Somebody said Goldsmith likes M^r & Mrs Thrale vastly – he never abuses them: no replies Johnson but he would be glad to hear they were parted tomorrow Morning, never to meet more.

Examples of Incredible Ignorance ○ We were talking of People who read awkwardly not knowing what they were about: Mr Johnson protested he knew two Lads at Pembroke who lived in the same Apartment, and one of them told him that the other had been reading Chillingworth for the last Week very diligently leaving a *Mark* always in the place he left off, which his *Chumm* moved a few Pages backward every Day, & so forced him unknown to himself to go over the same Ground without advancing one Jot or ever finding the Joke out. but this is not the best Story I have heard Mr Johnson tell of truly incredible Ignorance – here's a better.

Mr Johnson had two Boys recommended to his Care for

examination and further Instruction: the one was sixteen the other seventeen Years old: he found 'em very ready with their Grammatical & Mythological Learning – they had also read some English. Pray Gentlemen said Johnson do you know who dissolved the Monasteries in England? the eldest modestly replied he could not tell, – the other said *Jesus Christ*.

Perhaps he asked 'em in Words they did not understand – I was one Day examining a Lad* in the Roman History, and bid him tell me who *succeeded* Romulus – You might as well says Johnson ask him who *phlebotomized* Romulus – he would tell you as soon.

True Stories ↶ [Johnson] gave me the two following [stories] of his own Knowledge – & his Veracity cannot be questioned – he says a Story is valuable only as it is *true*.

When Garrick had acted Richard for the first three Times – some Overtures were made him by a Lady who sent a female Friend to him with Proposals of Marriage, mentioning her Fortune as high, and her Birth as noble. Mr Garrick and the Go-between had frequent Interviews which he confesses to have encouraged – but on a sudden she came no more – her Absence which was wholly unprovoked disturbed him a while but in a few Months he forgot it. Two Years after he met his Old Acquaintance in the Street; followed, and press'd her so tenderly and so irresistibly for an Explanation that after some Hesitation – Well Sir said She the Truth is the best Excuse – I will tell it you: – My Friend fell in Love with you playing King Richard, but seeing you since in the Character of the Lying Valet – you looked so – *shabby* (pardon me Sir) that it cured her of her Passion –

This Woman seems made up of Ignorance and Frenzy – did She take the Fellow for King Richard? and was it King Rich: She was in Love with? The Lady in the next Page is

[96]

still more to be stared at; & her husband still more than her – but She was *not* in Love, nor pretended so to be. I can much easier account for *her* Conduct, only the step was so criminal, and might have been the cause of still worse crimes.

Another True Story ↬ This Story was told me by Dr Johnson who had it from the Gentleman himself.

I was loitering says he about the Door of Queen's College when I saw a Chaise stop at the Angel Inn: I soon observed the Lady who came in it look out of the Window and in a quarter of an hour I was sent for to the Inn: I waited on the Lady who talked to me familiarly though with an odd Reserve which greatly affected me; and I saw from time to Time a starting Tear – Her Person was elegant tho' not striking, her Age thirty six; & her Voice had a softness which seemed the Consequence of Distress – we supt together & conversed quite freely, and her Understanding completed her Conquest – But what was my Astonishment when She gravely replied to my Courtship – Sir I sent for you on purpose – there are two Pillows on my Bed – You are at Liberty to follow me thither – & hastily retired as if shocked at what She had said. – I was strangely confounded, but resolved to comply. – Things were accordingly adjusted & in the morning I pressed her with the utmost Tenderness to tell me her Name and Condition – the former She would not disclose, though She insisted upon mine: She further informed me that She was a Married Woman, Wife to a Clergyman who had the sole possession of her Heart: that their Lives were rendered miserable by the want of a Child, as their Fortunes and Expectations were very high, that her Husband had agreed with her on this Expedient, & that if it answered to their hopes and Wishes I might assure myself of 50^£ p^r Ann if the Child was a Girl – 100^£ if a Boy. – the remittance to cease however if I ever revealed the Secret, or sought to discover more than She now thought fit to reveal – adding that we were *never, never* more to meet; that all enquiry on my Side would be fruitless, and that the Annuity should surely stop if ever I told the Adventures of the past Night – We parted with extreme Fondness on my Side, & some Tears on hers, & in ten Months Time I rec^d 100^£ without Letter or Note, which Pension was regularly continued for three Years: – My Vanity and Curiosity tempted me then to tell the Story, and hunt after the Lady – & I never more could see my Fairy Money, or hear of my Fairy Mistress.

Lichfield ◦ Speaking with Garrick of Johnson's partial fondness for Lichfield; he thinks Madam says he, that there is no such other Town – there is no Town replied I which ever produ[c]'d two such Men. – Oh replyed Garrick I am only the Gizzard Madam, trussed under the Turkey's Wing.

No Faint Denial ◦ The late Lord Huntingdon carried on in the reign of George 2^d a Secret Correspondence with the Son of James the 2^d commonly called the old Pretender; Sir Robert* charged his Lordship with so doing, & held a Paper in his hand while they talked. Sir said Lord Huntingdon I never saw the Man you mention: that replied Sir Robert Walpole is no *denial*; I know that you held your Conversations in the *Dark*, and the Letter in my hand contains the Proof of my Assertion. by this Discovery the skilful Minister secured at least Ld Huntingdon's Neutrality in all future Operations against the banished Family.

It was Mr Johnson who told me this strange Story, to inculcate a favourite Maxim of His, that when Truth is to be found we must not content ourselves with a faint or evasive denial.

Hawkins Browne ◦ Of Hawkins Browne* I have heard M^rs

[98]

Cholmondeley say that for the first hour – after Dinner – he was so *dull* there was no bearing him; for the second he was so *witty* there was no bearing him, and for the third, he was so *drunk* there was no bearing him.

Johnson said always that Browne's Conversation most resembled *mine*: it was says he, a stream of Sentiment – enlivened by Gaiety. I could not resist the Temptation of writing *that* down; ten to one I shall pretend to have forgotten it – & so write it over again in some other Volume of this Collection.

Garrick's Superiority ∽ Murphy loved Barry* & hated Garrick, he asserted to Mr Johnson one Day pretty roundly that Barry could actually do some things better than Garrick: what could he do better Sir says Johnson unless he had been set at the Door of a mean Auction Room with a long Pole in his hand to cry walk in Gentlemen; Nay replied Murphy briskly Mr Garrick might do that as well, & pick your Pocket into the bargain.

Johnson's First Meeting With Murphy ∽ The way Johnson & Murphy got acquainted was an odd one; Mr Murphy was ingaged in a Periodical Paper called I think the Grays Inn Journal, but he was in the Country with his Friend Foote & said he must go to Town to publish his Sheet for the Day: hang it says Foote can't you do it here & I'll send a Man & horse – tis but ten Miles – up to the printer: This was settled & Murphy impatient to join the Company & unwilling to pump his own Brains just then snatched up a French Journal that he saw lying about, translated a Story which he liked in it & sent it to press. When he came to Town two days after he soon found what he had done; that the Story was a Rambler written by Johnson, & translated into French; and that he had been doing it back again: he flew to Johnson's

Lodging, catched him making of Æther, told him the Truth and commenced an Acquaintance, which has lasted with mutual Esteem I suppose near twenty Years.

Too Much Love ∽ Seward* said he would not be married because he was not in Love – never wait for that said I; no do not Sir cries Johnson, too much Love does as much mischief among married People as too little; – Marriage is more a League at last of Friendship than of Love.

Rambling Sam ∽ I see Mr Johnson and I are abused in the Newspapers most ridiculously for *Rambling Sam* and the *witty Electionora*; one would wonder how such Stuff could seriously grieve any one; yet Cumyns the Quaker* died of a broken Heart occasioned by nothing more considerable, as Mr Johnson himself told me who had it from the Man as he lay on his deathbed.

Nothing under the Bed? ∽ We were speaking of theatrical Delusion, & whether any of the Audience ever were really even for a Moment perswaded that what they were either laughing or lamenting about was Matter of Fact: Johnson said every body knew fast enough that it was a *Show*, that they gave Money to see the Show, and that there was no Illusion in the Case – they knew he said that Mr Garrick & Mrs Cibber would take Care not to hurt themselves, when they pretended to kill or be killed, and denied that the Stage Artifices had any Chance to be supposed Realities by even the lowest Understanding in the place.

To contradict this Assertion Mr Murphy told the following Story, and appealed for the real Truth of it to Mr Thrale: – You knew says he Mrs Cantillon – was She an Ideot? – rather a *Sly Woman* than a foolish one, replied the other – well then continued Murphy with Mrs Cantillon I went to the Play once; it was to Othello – when we returned I asked her what She thought of it. – Why says She I think the Woman was a fool to lye a Bed there so quiet, & let the Black a moor throttle her: Was there nothing *under the Bed* She could have *throw'd* at him?

Translation of Anacreon ∽ Mr Johnson told me today that he had translated Anacreon's Dove, & as they were the first Greek Verses that had struck him when a Boy; so says he they continue to please me as well as any Greek Verses now I am Three score:† I hope added he, I have done them as well as Frank Fawkes;* – seeing me laugh at that – nay nay says he, Frank Fawkes has done them very finely. here however are Johnson's.

    Lovely Courier of the Sky
    Whence or whither dost thou fly?
    Scattring as thy Pinions play
    Liquid Fragrance all the way:
    Is it Business? is it Love?
    Tell me, Tell me, gentle Dove.

" " "Soft Anacreon's Vows I bear.
" " "Vows to Myrtale the fair;
" " "Grac'd with all that charms the heart
" " "Blushing Nature, smiling Art.
" " "Venus, courted with an Ode,
" " "On the Bard her Dove bestow'd,
" " "Vested with a Master's Right
" " "Now Anacreon rules my Flight.
" " "His the Letters which you see
" " "Weighty Charge consign'd to me,
" " "Think not yet my Service hard
" " "Joyless Task without Reward;

---

† 25: March Johnson said to me – so you have writ out my translation of the Dove in the *Thraliana* I warrant: I have so sd I; but have you mention'd says he that I intended doing it at sixteen, & never did, till I was 68, for that's most remarkable!

>   ""Smiling at my Master's Gates,
>   ""Freedom my Return awaits,
>   ""But the Liberal Grant in vain
>   ""Tempts me to be wild again;
>   ""Can a prudent Dove decline
>   ""Blissful Bondage such as mine?
>   ""Over Hills and Fields to roam
>   ""Fortune's Guest, without a home,
>   ""Under Leaves to hide ones head,
>   ""Slightly shelter'd coarsely fed?
>   ""Now my better Lot bestows
>   ""Sweet Repast, and soft repose:
>   ""Now the generous Bowl I sip
>   ""As it leaves Anacreon's Lip,
>   ""Void of Care, and free from dread
>   ""From his Fingers snatch his Bread,
>   ""Then with luscious Plenty gay
>   ""Round his Chamber dance and play,
>   ""Or from Wine as Courage springs,
>   ""O'er his Face extend my Wings;
>   ""And when Feast and Frolick tire
>   ""Drop asleep upon his Lyre.
>   ""This is all; – be quick and go,
>   ""More than all thou canst not know;
>   ""Let me now my Pinions ply
>   ""I have chatter'd like a Pye. –""

A Broken Nose ~ Such – says Mr Johnson was the Success of Fielding's Amelia, that a second Edition was prepared in the Afternoon of the Day in which the first was published; but on the next Morning it was contradicted; for by that Time the Town had found out that Amelia had performed all her Wonders with a broken Nose, which Fielding had forgotten to cure, & had broken indeed for no other Reason than to impress himself with an Idea of his favourite Wife, who had once met with a similar Accident, & whose Character he had meant to exhibit under the Name of Amelia: thus did this oddity spoyl the Sale of one of the first Performances in the World of its Kind; merely because it was an Error obvious to all Mankind – *a la porteè de chacun* as the French express it; & thus will one *Moral* Fault – as *Lying* for example tarnish the most splendid Character, & counteract the Influence of the warmest Virtues. – This I wrote down one Day from Johnson's Mouth.

Congreve's Mourning Bride ↬ I have heard Johnson say that there was no Series of Verses in any English Tragedy so sublime & striking as the Passage in Congreve's Mourning Bride: beginning thus

> How reverend is the Face of Yon tall Pile!

but Johnson was more a Man of Imagination than Passion, the Distresses of high Life affected him but little; & Lear's cursing his Daughter which makes so many People shudder, took no hold of him at all I think.

The Ruling Passion ↬ Johnson says that Pope's Ideas of the ruling Passion were not well discriminated at all, but mixed with notions of another Sort; the Courtier's Exit is in the performance of a Ceremony & who can call Ceremony a Passion?

Seraphick Beer ↬ Mr Johnson says – speaking of People's different notions concerning Humour – that one grave old Fellow of a College said of another – my Friend was particularly happy in his Fancy, & eminent for Arch Reparties; being for example ask'd one Day His opinion of some College Beer, he answered humourously that it was Seraphick and there was none like it.

A Hexagon Defined ↬ Mr Johnson & I were distilling some

Pot herbs one Day for Amusement in a Glass Retort over a Lamp, & we observed all the Bubbles to be hexagonal a Thing we could give no Account of. Mr Johnson however took Occasion from that Circumstance to tell me that a Hexagon is that form which contains most Space excepting the Circle, which however not admitting of Coalescence, loses more by being added to another Circle, than it gains by the Superiority of Shape. a Hexagon is therefore on the whole the most capacious form. I have since this was told me, reflected that the Cells of a Honeycomb are always hexagonal; & it comes in my Head that Queen Dido when She cut her Bulls hide to build Carthage, set the slips hexagonally: I'm sure that I have read that She did so. Why so? if the Circle contains most Space.

Reason the Only Source of Happiness ∽ I was mentioning the happiness of Enthusiastick Piety, & observing that no people possessed so much real Felicity as they whose hearts were warmed with that only valuable Cordial: Let us remember however said Johnson that Reason is the only Source of happiness to reasonable Beings; There is doubtless an Enjoyment in straining Imagination to Madness, & so there is in spurring up the Senses to Brutality: but as both are contrary to God's apparent Intention, so both are perversions of his Gifts, & criminal before his Sight.

Public Life is Best ∽ Johnson, who thinks the vacuity of Life the source of all ye Passions, says it is certainly so both with regard to Love & Friendship: In the Hurry of a Battle or the Distresses of a Siege, the Pressure of Poverty or the invasions of Pain, a Mistress or a Friend have certainly small Chance to be remembred; & even in the lesser Tumults of Amusement & Dissipation there is but little Leisure for Attachment and of Course for Reflexion; Public Life he therefore holds to be safest & best for Youth of both Sexes – no harm says he, can possibly be done before so many Witnesses.

Making Vows ↬ People have a strange Propensity to making Vows on trifling Occasions, a Trick one would not think of; but I once caught my Husband at it, and have since then been suspicious that 'tis oftener done than believ'd. – For Example Mr Thrale & I were driving thro' E: Grinstead and found the Inn we used to put up at destroyed by Fire: he express'd great Uneasiness, & I still kept crying why can we not go to the other Inn? – tis a very good house – here is no Difficulty in the Case: all this while Mr Thrale grew violently impatient endeavoured to bribe the Post Boy to go on to the next Post Town &c but in vain; till pressed by Enquiries and Solicitations he could no longer elude, he confessed to me that he had sworne an oath or made a Vow I forget which, 17 Years before; never to set his Foot within those Doors again, having had some Fraud practised on him by a Landlord who then kept the house but had been dead long enough ago. – when I heard this all was well; I desired him to sit in the Chaise, while the Horses were changed: & walked into the house myself to get some Refreshment the while.

Mr Johnson told me he knew a Lady who had such a habit of lingering, that She never could get herself dressed for Dinner, till She had made a *Vow* to do so.

Pope's Cough ↬ I have heard Mr Johnson remark that nobody could ever relate any Thing that Pope *said*; we were settling it that he made no figure in Conversation, when Mrs Montagu recollecting herself observed that She had never heard him speak indeed, but She once had heard him cough: you heard then Madam says Johnson as much from him as anybody ever did.

Sublime Verses ～ Johnson says the following 8 Lines of Burney are actually sublime – they are the End of a dull Copy of Verses enough, but the Lines themselves are most excellent.

> The Monster Death keeps full in Sight,
> And puts the Faery Hope to flight;
> Blackens th' Horizon all around
> And points to the Abyss profound.
>
> 'Gainst Nature's Laws 'tis vain to plead
> I see the Joys of Life recede;
> And all its Prospects fade away
> Amidst the Horrors of Decay.

An Odd Thing ～ Mr Johnson told me an odd Thing today: Robinson the Primate of Ireland had said to Mrs Montagu that there was a District not far from Dublin called Fingal where the People still spoke the old English Language; and says he they will even to this Hour take up Chaucer & laugh at what we cannot understand. Now see says Mr Johnson how little Wit is wanted to *lye with*! The Language of Chaucer was never the common Language of the Multitude, nor could people of the Rank he mentioned *ever* understand it: Chaucer was written in the high Court Dialect of his Time, & even at that Time totally unintelligible to the Vulgar.

Johnson's Incredulity ～ The Weather is still offensively hot – we shall have more Thunder I suppose – the Thunder & Lightning last April when I went to Brighthelmstone – *to Mr Scrase* – was so violent as to break & set on Fire a large Bottle full of Spirits in Mrs Lucas's Window, at the moment I was there, so I saw it; I could not however make Mr Johnson believe the Fact.

Mr Johnson's Incredulity amounts almost to Disease; he will not believe that a Haystack was ever burned, or a

Waggon ever set on fire by the Friction of the one I mean, or the Fermentation of the other: he is a sad Mortal to carry a Wonder to, for says he I am of poor dear Dr Goldsmith's Mind – he looked for new Thoughts a while but was at last convinced as he told me – that whatever was new was false.

A Head in Hornsey Wood ∽ A Story told this Year in the Newspapers† about a Man's Head seen in Hornsey Wood is a very curious one; 'tis well authenticated I hear, but Johnson don't believe it.

Everybody like a Dish ∽ We were diverting ourselves with Goldsmith's Idea of every body's being like some Dish of meat we agreed that

Johnson should be – –	Haunch of Venison
Pepys – – –	a Perigord Pye.
Bodens – – –	a Piece of Sturgeon.
Mrs Montagu – – –	Soup – à la *Reine*.
Sophy Streatfield – –	White Fricassee
Mrs Byron – – –	Provincial Toast.
Seward – – –	a Ham.
Dr Burney – – –	a dish of fine Green Tea.
Mrs Smith – – –	an Aspique.
Tom Cotton – – –	Water-Suchy.
Lort – – –	Beef Steaks.
Mrs Pepys – – –	Boil'd Whiting.
Fanny Brown – – –	Landskip in Jelly.

to these Mr Johnson desired he might add the following

My Master* – – –	Roast Beef
My M^rs* – – –	a Gallina

† It was a Man set by advice of some Quack Doctor in an Earth Bath, & terrified a Boy into temporary Madness who walking early in the Wood one Morn^g saw a live Head on the Ground its Eyes moving & no Body visible – I see not how such an object on such a Mind should have less Effect.

  Miss Burney – – – a Woodcock
  & Sir Philip Jennings – a Roasted Sweetbread.

The Finest Tragic Scene ∽ Johnson says the finest Tragic Scene in our Language, for Drama Sentiment, Language, Power over the heart, & every Requisite for Theatre or Closet, is the Tomb Scene in the Mourning Bride.
 I think, that trying to be *every* thing it escapes being *anything*.

Don Quixote ∽ No Book was ever so popular as Don Quixote; The Classics themselves are more confined in Fame: Don Quixote is the Book for high & for low, Indocti doctiqu[e] – French, English, Germans, Parents & Children, Servants and Masters: in every Nation Quixotism is proverbial, & the Don Naturalized.† Biva pues, Cervantes!

Champagne ∽ Johnson says Women who will not work & cannot play at Cards must drink Drams of necessity. I love work dearly, and I can bear Cards well enough now & then; sure I shall never take to Dram drinking – I hate every sort of Drink at present but Toast & Water, tho' there is one other Liquor I could *delight in* and only one. Champagne.

Johnson's Laziness ∽ I have a great Aversion to a Difficulty Maker – a Man who if one asks him to write a Letter of Solicitation will make Enquiries & hunt after Scruples – let a Man oblige *me* at a Word or I will ask him no more. For promptness of Expedient, Activity in removing Obstacles,

---

 † Mr Johnson & I betted a Wager about this Position; I said there would be found three Servants out of our eighteen who had read Don Quixot & he said not. – I however came off more than Winner, Old Nurse, the Nursery Maid, the Dairy Maid, my own Maid & Mr Thrales Valet had all read the Book, & related some Adventure out on't; for that Johnson insisted on, as a Proof of their having read it; & he objected to the Windmills as a too popular & common Story to be considered as corroboratory.

X THE SUMMER HOUSE AT STREATHAM

Solicitude to oblige, & Alacrity to dispatch the Business, – give me Sir Thomas Mills. – Johnson is admirable at giving Counsel – no Man sees his Way better, but he will not stir to do anything –

> His Pride in Reas'ning not in Acting lies.

besides that he has Principles of Laziness and can be indolent by Rule: to hinder your Death or procure you a Dinner; – I mean if starving – he will set about most vigorously, and do it with all possible Effect; but to obtain a Vote in a Society, repay a Compliment which would be of future Utility, write a Letter requesting a Favour from a distant Friend – or such things; no Force moves him, nor no Tenderness can induce. – What good will it do the Man says he? Dearest Lady let's have no more on't.

A Reply to Garrick ↢ Says Garrick to Johnson why did not you make me a Tory? you love to make people Tories. – Says Johnson to Garrick pulling a Handful of Half pence out of his Wastecoat pocket – Why did not the King make these – Guineas?

Nobody but Grotius ↢ We were saying that

> " "No one would change his Neighbour for himself – " "

in short that no Man would change himself – that is his own Character all together, person Mind – Chance for Eternity tout ensemble with any other Man or Woman living or dead.

Johnson said he would change with nobody but Hugo Grotius.* Burney rather wished to be Metastasio, – Boswell indeed desired to be Shakespear; but my Master – happy Man! desired only to remain *himself* for as many Years as he had already lived – here now are various & peculiar Modifications of Pride! every Man is so much the Standard of Excellence to himself, that he chuses that Character which

[110]

is only *his own* amplified & exalted – thus Johnson wished to be still *more* a Wit a Critick & Philosopher.

Johnson's Uncles ∽ What makes you love Sir Richard Jebb so, my Dear Mistress says Johnson to me one Evening? he is open & confiding says I, & tells me Stories of his Uncles & his Cousins, & I love such Talk for my part – Nay replies Mr Johnson if you love Stories of Relations – I can fit you.

I had an Uncle Cornelius Ford my Mother's Brother continued he, who on a Journey stopt to read an Inscription upon a Stone he saw – which was set up as he then found in honour of a Man who had leaped a certain Leap thereabouts, the extent of wch was specified on the inscription – why says my Uncle I can leap it in my Boots – & he did accordingly leap it in his Boots. – I had likewise an Uncle Andrew (my Father's Brother) says Dr Johnson – who kept the Ring in Smithfield a whole Year – (where they wrestled & boxed) – and never was thrown or conquered – here says he are Uncles for you! – if that's the way to your Heart.

No Man A Hero to his Valet ∽ It appears to me that no Man can live his Life quite thro', without being at *some* period of it under the Dominion of *some* Woman – Wife Mistress or Friend.

Pope & Swift, were softened by the Smiles of Patty Blount & Stella; & our stern Philosopher Johnson trusted me about the Years 1767 or 1768 – I know not which just now – with a Secret far dearer to him than his Life:* such however is his nobleness, & such his partiality, that I sincerely believe he has never since that Day regretted his Confidence, or ever looked with less kind Affection on her who had him in her Power. – Uniformly great is the Mind of that incomparable Mortal; & well does he contradict the Maxim of Rochefoucault, that no Man is a Hero to his Valet de Chambre. –

Johnson is more a Hero to me than to any one – & I have been more to him for Intimacy, than ever was any Man's Valet de Chambre.

A Woman's Power ↝ Says Johnson a Woman has *such* power between the Ages of twenty five and forty five, that She may tye a Man to a post and whip him if She will.† I thought they must begin earlier & leave off sooner, but he says that 'tis not *Girls* but *Women* who inspire the violent & lasting passions – Cleopatra was Forty three Years old when Anthony lost the World for her.

A Caricatura of Potter ↝ Johnson has been diverting himself with imitating Potter's Æschylus in a translation of some Verses of Euripides – he has translated them seriously besides, & given them Burney for his History of Musick. here are the Burlesque ones – but they are a *Caricatura* of Potter whose Verses are obscure enough too.

> Err shall they not, who resolute explore
> Times gloomy backward with judicious Eyes;
> And scanning right the practices of yore,
> Shall deem our hoar progenitors unwise.
>
> They to the Dome where Smoke with curling Play
> Announc'd the Dinner to the Regions round;
> Summon'd the Singer blythe, and Harper gay,
> And aided Wine with dulcet streaming Sound.
>
> The better use of Notes or sweet or shrill
> By quivring string or modulated Wind;
> Trumpet or Lyre to their harsh Bosoms chill,
> Admission ne'er had sought or could not find –

† This he knew of him self was *literally* and *strictly* true I am sure.

>   Oh send them to the Sullen Mansions dun,
>   Her baleful Eyes where Sorrow rolls around;
>   Where gloom-enamour'd Mischief dreads the Sun
>   And Murder – all blood-bolter'd – schemes the Wound.
>
>   When Cates luxuriant pile the spacious dish,
>   And purple Nectar glads the festive Hour,
>   The Guest without a Want, without a Wish,
>   Can yield no Room to Musick's soothing powr.

Poor Potter! he does write strange unintelligible Verses to be sure, but I think none as bad as these neither. Mr Johnson's *real* Translation of this bit of Euripides I have not; but it is to be printed in Burney's second Volume of his History of Musick, so no matter for writing it out if one had it. – 'tis very elegant I remember.

Dr Percy Mocked ∽

>   The tender Infant meek and mild
>   Fell down upon a Stone;
>   The Nurse took up the squealing Child
>   But yet the Child squeal'd on.

These Verses which were meant to make Fun of Dr Percy's Poem called the Hermit of Warkworth got about, & made Percy angry but he soon came to himself.

Learn One Thing Well ∽ Johnson says that the best way for every Man at setting out in Life is to learn some one Thing well: the Man of general Knowledge says he, is never wanted; he who can cure Pain is necessary when one is diseased, he who [can] extricate one from a Law Suit is useful when his Neighbours are entangled, but the Reasoner & the Traveller tho' entertaining Companions are not often thought on, merely because they are not ever wanted.

A Gay Gown ∽ I had a Grave coloured Gown on today, & Johnson reproved me for calling old Age too soon; a gay Gown in a Morning said I is out of Rule – but thou art so little my Love he replied, that Rules may be superseded in Your Case – What! have not *all Insects* gay Colours? He thought himself expiring & was amazingly cross.

Viva Johnson! ∽ Mr Johnson was saying that if any Man shewed an Inclination to waste his health & Fortune by Riot & Extravagance, all his Friends would agree to encourage him in his Course; but if a Man shew'd a Desire to save his Money & live abstemiously, every Acquaintance would throw some Rub in his way: – so says he while a Man continues active in his own Affairs, & useful in those of others; he is called, or thought at least, a busy officious disagreeable Fellow; but as soon as he fancies himself sick, & proposes *Retirement*, every Friend helps fetch a Pillow, and runs to *tuck* the good *Gentleman in*. – never says he take to your Room while you can be in Company; never take to your Bed while you can sit up: the Nephews & Nieces will make haste to hide you else, & by preventing your Wishes with Cups of warm Jelly &c. bribe you to sit still, while they take Advantage of your Retreat.

Viva Johnson! how true all this is!

Strange Connections in this Odd World ∽ I have an odd Power of working myself up into artificial Spirits: one Day in the first Week of April 1777. when I was vexed & frighted out of my Wits because of the Accident – if one may call it such – that befell our Business, when Mr Thrale was agonizing with Apprehension, & I was within a Month or two of lying In, & setting out for Money & Advice to dear Mr Scrase at Brighthelmstone; I remember Boswell dining here: we†

† by the Word *We* I mean Johnson & myself – my Master looked then as he does now, like a Man Woe-begone.

talked, we rattled, we flashed, we made extempore Verses, we did so much that at last Mr Boswell said why Mrs Thrale (says he) you are in most riotous Spirits to-day – So I am reply'd I gaily, & actually ran out of the Room to cry – his observation went so to my Heart.

How many Times has this great, this formidable Doctor Johnson kissed my hand, ay & my foot too upon his knees!

Strange Connections there are in this odd World!† his with me is mere *Interest* tho'; – he loves Miss Reynolds better.

Hester's New Hat ⌇ Hester was deliberating whether She should put on her fine new dressed hat to dine at Mrs Montagus next Fryday – *do* my Darling says Johnson.

> Wear the Gown, & wear the Hat,
> Snatch your pleasures while they last;
> Hadst thou nine Lives like a Cat,
> Soon those nine Lives would be past.

Towns Ending in Chester ⌇ Johnson says that all Names of Towns ending in Chester were Roman Stations – Castrum. London was British indeed, & named by Tacitus, the Rest are all Saxon.

Verses to Sir John Lade ⌇ Johnson – in a fit of frolicksome Gaiety has sent me some comical Verses of Congratulation to Sir John Lade* upon his coming of Age: tis amazing how airily & pleasantly he celebrates the Joys of a young Spendthrift heir – himself being now seventy one Years old – here they are

> Long expected one and Twenty
> Lingring Year at last is flown;

† a dreadful & little suspected Reason for *ours* God knows – but the Fetters & Padlocks* will tell Posterity the Truth.

Pride and Pleasure, Pomp & Plenty,
Great Sir John are now your own.

Loosen'd from the Minor's Tether,
Free to mortgage or to sell,
Wild as Wind, and light as Feather,
Bid the Slaves of Thrift farewell.

Call the Betsys, Kates, and Jennys,
All the Names that laugh at Care;
Lavish of your Grandsire's Guineas,
Show the Spirit of an Heir.

All that prey on Vice or folly
Joy to see their Quarry fly;
Here the Gameſter light & Jolly,
There the Lender grave and sly.

Wealth Sir John was made to wander,
Let it wander as it will:
See the Jockey, see the Pander,
Bid them come and take their fill.

When the bonny Blade carouses
Pockets full, and Spirits high;
What are Acres? what are Houses?
Only dirt, or wet or dry.

If the Guardian or the Mother
Tell the woes of wilful Waſte
Scorn their Counsel, scorn their pother,
You can hang or drown at laſt.

Solander's Conversation ↬ I was commending Solander's* Conversation — He may says Mr Johnson deserve all your Praise, but you do not know that he does, — nor I neither: the pump answers well to be sure, but the Stream may for ought I can tell flow from a Reservoir only, & not from a Spring. Let's ſtay till we have been longer acquainted.

[116]

Death of a Jamaica Gentleman ∽ A Jamaica Gentleman died; – he was a very wicked Fellow – He will not says Johnson find much difference where he is gone; either in the Climate, or in the Company.

Burke & Fox ∽ They were talking of Burke & Fox; the first has more Bullion Says Mr Johnson, but the other coins faster. this might be said I think of Mrs Montagu and me.

Psalmanazar ∽ Psalmanazar* wrote the Cosmogony, and the History of the Jews after his Conversion; how odd that he should quote the Formosan Opinions therefore as corroborative of some Hypothesis; which he certainly does, and with a Touch of his old Effrontery too. see Page 84: Vol: 1. Universal History.

I have heard Mr Johnson say Psalmanazar was the *best* Man he ever knew. – if he play'd these Tricks however, he was not the *Fair* Penitent.

Riding in a Carriage ∽ How fond some People are of riding in a Carriage! those most I think who had from beginning least Chance of keeping one; Johnson doats on a Coach, so do many People indeed:

Roosts for Ignorance ∽ Susan and Sophy are come home, grown immoderately, and very clever Girls: for drawing, Music, & School Accomplishments – *very clever indeed*: besides Taste for Poetry, Skill in Geography, and a Thousand *Appliqués* which however take no Root I have a Notion, for the common Sense lies fallow, all the while these Cornflowers continue to grow; & I sometimes doubt whether exteriors are not at last dearly purchased by the utter darkness with regard to

That which before us lies in daily Life – Milton.

that surrounds a Ladies Boarding School: – Roosts for Ignorance as Johnson says. When they come home they must be taught to think; a Lesson never learned in youth but of one's Mother.

A Sick Man A Scoundrel ↝ Mr Johnson has such an Aversion to the Liberties taken by sick People with their surrounding Friends, that it has greatly blunted his Compassion – it is so difficult says he for a sick Man not *to be a Scoundrel*: Oh! set the Pillows soft – Mr Grumbler is coming – Oh! let no Air in for the World, Mr Grumbler will catch Cold;† this perpetual Preference is so offensive, where the Privileges of Illness are supported by Wealth; and nourished by Dependance; that one cannot wonder a rough mind is revolted by them.

The drollery is, that being habitually watchful against such behaviour, he is sometimes ready to suspect it in himself, & when one asks him how he does – will often reply – "'ready to become a Scoundrel dear Madam, with a little more spoiling, you will make *me* a Rascal very soon.'"

The Welfare of Relations ↝ His Desire of doing good was however not lessened by his Sensibility of receiving Pain; he would have made an Ill Man well by any Expence or fatigue of his own, sooner than any of the Canters. Canter indeed he was none; he would forget to ask people after their Relation's Welfare, & say in excuse that he knew they did not care, for why should they? every body had as much as they could do in this World to care for themselves; & no

† He did not learn these Notions from Mr Thrale's sick Bed: *he* bears all Illness with astonishing Tranquillity, & a sort of manly sullenness which tho' not amiable compels Respect. he claims no Indulgence, he desires no Pity – and sits down to a Surgeon's incision-Knife, exactly as he sits down to a Barber's Razor. no Mr Grumbler in his Character or Composition.

Leisure to *think* of their Neighbour's Distresses, however they might take Delight in *talking* of them.

Such sort of *Mandevillian* Doctrine, did not gain him Friends to be sure; but his high Reputation for Piety & Virtue hindered it from doing him any real harm: poor dear Doctor Collier owed much of his Ruin to such Conversation, but Johnson knew better than ever to leave a Company with Impressions to his Disadvantage – he valued the World's good Word exceedingly – & said so – while he appeared to set it at Defiance.

Johnson at Oxford ↜ I have heard Mr Johnson relate how very insolently he behaved at Oxford when a Youth; how he went *one* Day to his Tutour, & finding him no *Scholar*, went no more: in a Week's Time, Jordan met and enquired of him what he [had] been doing – "'"sliding on the Ice"'" was the Reply, so he turned away with disdain. They bore it from me though says he with wonderful Gentleness, and surprising Acquiescence as I have thought since – *Ay*! *why the same Inferiority* quoth H: L: T. no no Mistress; I won't have that Story so alluded to† – but thus much is true enough; that no Man leaps into deep Water, unless he knows he can swim. Upon this Principle no doubt when he made his first Declamation he wrote over but one Copy, & gave it to the Tutour at the bottom of the Hall, and not having had time to get above half of it by heart, trusted to his own Powers for present supply: these answered his purpose so well however, that he found himself at no Loss, and came off with prodigious Applause. – the Gentleman could *swim* pretty well it seems.

† The Story alluded to is of Miss Langton, who had grossly insulted her Aunt Dury: when the Peace makers begun reconciling them, they urged the Patience with which the Lady had long endured her Arrogance – To be sure replies the Girl – *the same stupidity* which provoked my Passion, helped her to bear it I suppose – that's all.

Johnson & the Hurricane ∽ Mr Johnson believes nothing – the Hurricane which has torn Barbadoes to pieces, & is related so pathetically in the Gazette – " "not true Madam depend upon't – People so delight to fill their Mouthes with big Words, and their Minds with a Wonder." " did you ever says I believe anything reported? " "never scarcely, & I *have* been deceived! for I did not give Credit a long Time to the Earthquake at Lisbon." "

This is another mode of making Enemies however; and what Sport is there in flinging People's Opinions back upon them so? Mr Sharp the Surgeon was quite shocked today at Dr. Johnson's persisting in the Falsehood of a Calamity that shocked every one else. Oh says I, Mr Johnson does not resemble Solomon more than David: for he *says in his haste – all Men are Lyars*.

If I was to tell Mr Johnson that Jersey was taken by the French he would not believe me, if I was to tell him I saw my Mother or my Grandmother last Night he would believe me; what an odd thing is the human Mind! – Surely the taking Jersey is more probable than the reappearance of a dead Friend.

Seldom Wanted ∽ I was saying to Dr Johnson that Virtue alone would not make old Age respectable, for that was insisted on: & that the Quiet Character he commended so, would in very advanced Life sink into a poor Thing. I had old Mrs Shelley in my head – Ah no replies he, such folks as you & I are seldom wanted dear Mistress, & therefore of little Value – the Knife & fork will beat the Buckler & Target at the *long Run*;

Zachary Pearce ∽ Mr Johnson was saying the other Day that Zachary Pearce* when he had lost his Wife, with whom he had lived a vast many years; drank one Glass on the Evening of her Funeral saying among his Friends

""Here's to the pious Memory of her that is departed!""

and then never named her more.

Judge Impey ↜ Johnson had (as a good Man) – a great Aversion to Scripture Allusions as bordering on profane-[ne]ss; yet when I exclaimed on the Sight of Impey* a low Fellow presented at Court when he was going Judge to East India – What dost thou here Elijah! Johnson sate & laughed without speaking a word.

Death of Levett ↜ Doctor Johnson has been writing Verses on his old Inmate Mr Levett he tells me: that poor Creature was 84 or 85 years old this Winter, when after an uninterrupted Series of Health he died suddenly by a Spasm or Rupture of some of the Vessels of the Heart. he lived with Johnson as a sort of *necessary Man*, or Surgeon to the wretched Household he held in Bolt Court; where Blind Mrs Williams, Dropsical Mrs Desmoulines, Black Francis & his White Wife's Bastard with a wretched Mrs White, and a Thing that he called Poll; shared his Bounty, & increased his Dirt. Levett used to bleed one, & blister another, & be very useful, tho' I believe disagreable to all: he died while his Patron was with me in Harley Street – & very sorry he was – in his way of being sorry – & he wrote these Verses

1.
Condemn'd to Hope's delusive Mine
As on we toil from Day to day;
By sudden Blast, or slow decline,
Our social Comforts drop away.

2.
Well tried thro' many a varying Year,
See Levett to the Grave descend;

Officious, Innocent – Sincere –
    Of every friendless Name the Friend.

3.

Yet still he fills Affection's Eye,
    Obscurely wise, and coarsely kind;
Nor letter'd Arrogance deny
    Thy Praise to Merit unrefin'd.

4.

When fainting Nature call'd for aid
    And hov'ring Death prepar'd the blow;
His vigrous Remedy display'd
    The Pow'r of Art without the Show.

5.

In Misery's darkest Caverns known
    His useful Care was ever nigh:
Where hopeless Anguish pour'd his Groan
    And lonely Want retir'd to dye.

6.

No Summons mock'd by chill delay,
    No petty Gain disdain'd by Pride;
The modest Wants of every day,
    The Toil of every day supplied.

7.

His Virtues walk'd their narrow Round,
    Nor made a Pause nor left a Void;
And sure th' Eternal Master found
    The single Talent well employ'd.

8.

The busy Day, the peaceful Night
    Unfelt, uncounted glided by;
His Frame was firm, his Pow'rs were bright,
    Tho' now his eightieth Year was nigh.

9.
> Then with no Throbs of fiery Pain
> No cold Gradations of Decay;
> Death broke at once the vital Chain,
> And freed his Soul the nearest way.

Measureless Delight ~ And so says Johnson I guess Miss Burney's Book* concludes by leaving her heroine Cecilia in measureless delight. I wonder when any body ever experiences measureless delight: *I* never did I'm sure except the first Evening I spent Teste a Teste with Molly Aston* – so when we parted I made a Distich; for Molly was a Whig, & talked all about Liberty: here's my Distich, you may write it down if you will.

> Liber ut esse velim suasisti pulchra Maria,
> Ut maneam liber pulchra Maria vale.*

The Skaiters ~ Verses written under some Figures skaiting.

> Sur un mince Chrystal L'Hyver conduit leurs Pas,
> Le Precipice est sous la Glace;
> Tel est de nos Plaisirs la legere Surface,
> Glissez Mortels – n'appuyez pas.

Translated by H: L: T.

> Thus o'er the dangerous Gulph below
> Is Pleasure's slippery Surface spread;
> On tender Steps – with Caution go,
> They soonest sink, who boldest tread.

By Dr Johnson.

> O'er Ice the rapid Skaiter flies
> With Sport above & Death below;
> Where Mischief lurks in gay Disguise
> Thus lightly touch & quickly go.

Another by Dr Johnson.

> On crackling Ice o'er Gulphs profound,
> With nimble Glide the Skaiters play;
> O'er treach'rous Pleasure's flow'ry Ground
> Thus lightly skim – and haste away.

Miss Burney's Novel ∽ Wyndham* & Johnson were talking of Miss Burney's new Novel – 'Tis far superior to Fielding's, says Mr Johnson; her Characters are nicer discriminated, and less prominent, Fielding could describe a Horse or an Ass, but he never reached to a Mule.

Johnson & the Orange Peel ∽ I used to tell him in Jest that his Biographers would be at a Loss concerning some Orange Peel he used to keep in his pocket,* and many a Joke we had about the Lives that would be published: rescue me out of all their hands My dear, & do it *yourself* said he: "'Taylor Adams & Hector will furnish you with juvenile Anecdotes, & Baretti will give you all the rest that you have not already – for I think Baretti is a Lyar only when he speaks of himself.'" Oh! said I Baretti told me Yesterday that you got by Heart six Pages of Machiavel's History once, & repeated 'em thirty Years afterwards Word for Word. O why this indeed is a *gross* Lye, says Johnson – I never read the Book at all. Baretti too told me of *you* (said I) that you once kept 16 Cats in your Chamber, & y^t they scratch'd your Legs to such a degree, you were forced to use Mercurial Plaisters for some Time after. Why this (replied Johnson) is an unprovoked Lye indeed: I thought the Fellow would not have broken thro' divine & Human Laws thus, to make Puss his Heroine – but I see I was mistaken.

Upon Chester Wall ∽ Chester Wall put me in mind of poor dear Dr Johnson who said one day very drolly; *now have I known my Mistress sixteen Years*, & never saw her out of Humour yet – except once upon Chester Wall.

XI DR JOHNSON

George III's Madness ↬ I don't believe the King has ever been much worse than poor Dr Johnson was, when he fancied that eating an Apple would make him drunk.

Sir Joshua Grows Old ↬ I saw Sir Joshua Reynolds last night at the Byng's; we hardly looked at each other – yet I see he grows old, & is under the Dominion of a *Niece*: Oh! that is poor Work indeed for Sir Joshua Reynolds. I always told Johnson that they overrated that Man's mental Qualities; he replied Everybody loves Reynolds except *you*.

Her Anecdotes ↬ Our Letters – that is the Correspondence between Johnson & myself will come out now very soon: I *know* of only six professed Enemies who are determined to write against the Book, but there are doubtless six and twenty of whom I know nothing. Well! Johnson always said that nothing could sink a Book except its own dulness – if so – why Cry you mercy Enemies – we fall by our own Hands.

Filial Fondness ↬ Mrs Byron is now old and infirm, & apparently in her last Stage of Existence – Lady Wilmot's Death last Year broke her up, & She c^d never recover to be what She was before. but not a Daughter ever goes near her, & the only Son that should be her Comfort, is in India.

In Italy 'tis otherwise: more filial piety; less spurning at the common Ties of Nature. We are *too much* civilized, & have refined away original Feelings strangely. Johnson always maintained that no such Attachment naturally subsisted and used to chide me for *fancying* that I loved my Mother. Kemble now contents himself with saying that maternal Instinct *does* subsist – but Filial fondness *never*: Dr Johnson said Mr Thrale was sorry for his only Son's Death, just as a Man frets when he sees his fine new-built House tumble down, – but *no more*. he denied parental Feelings entirely; & said the Cow low'd after the Calf, only because it eased her of the Pain in the Udder: was She constantly kept dry-milked said he, you would hear her low no more.

Pet Names for Children ↩ Doctor Johnson who was never wrong hardly, was seldom more right than when he warned people against giving their Children Pet Names, or Sousbriquets as the French call them.

Not to Stare About ↩ Rousseau is not like Johnson when he thinks a mute & sublime Admiration of his worke the best Worship of the Creator, altho' that Admiration should excite no Act of any sort, but end wholly in itself – Johnson thought that God Almighty sent us here *to do* something, – not merely to *stare about*.

* * *

NOTES

page
3 – Only four of Mrs Thrale's eleven children survived into maturity. They were Hester Maria, Susanna Arabella, Sophia and Cecilia Margaretta.

4 – Arthur Murphy (1727-1805), actor and author. He wrote *An Essay on the Life and Genius of Samuel Johnson*, 1792.

4 – Rev. Cornelius Ford (1694-1731). According to Mrs Thrale, Johnson 'always spoke of him with tenderness' – *Anecdotes of the Late Samuel Johnson, LL.D. During the Last Twenty Years of His Life* by Hester Lynch Piozzi, 1786.

5 – Catherine Chambers (1709-1767) was not Johnson's nurse. Mrs Thrale is also wrong in suggesting that he did not see Miss Chambers before she died. For an account of his last visit to her see Johnson's *Prayers and Meditations*, 1785, one of the best short pieces of writing in English literature.

6 – *De Veritate Religionis Christianae* by Hugo Grotius, 1627. (See also note p. 110 below.)

6 – Dr John Taylor (1711-1788) was one of Johnson's oldest and closest friends. He went to school with him at Lichfield. Johnson frequently stayed with Taylor at his grand home at Ashbourne, Derbyshire.

6 – Dr Richard Bathurst (d. 1762), an unsuccessful physician. 'Johnson hardly ever spoke of Bathurst without tears in his eyes' – Arthur Murphy, *op. cit.*

7 – *The Rambler*. A series of over 200 essays by Johnson published as a twice-weekly periodical between 1750 and 1752.

8 – *The Idler*. Title of a series of essays written by Johnson for a weekly periodical between 1758 and 1760.

8 – Guiseppe Baretti (1719-1789), critic and grammarian. Came to England in 1750. He was charged with murder in 1769 after he stabbed a man who assaulted him for striking a street-walker. He was acquitted. Tutor to the Thrales' eldest daughter, Hester, he composed his *Early Phraseology for the Use of Young Ladies*, 1775 (with a preface by Johnson) for her benefit. Left Streatham under a cloud in 1776 and subsequently attacked Mrs Thrale, describing her as a 'frontless female who goes now by the mean appellation of Piozzi' – *European Magazine*, May 1788.

8 – Rev. William Dodd (1729-1777) was hanged in 1777 for forging the name of the Earl of Chesterfield on a bond worth £4,000. Johnson vainly appealed for clemency to the Lord Chancellor and others.
8 – In 1777 Johnson wrote a prologue for Hugh Kelly's play, *A Word for the Wise*.
10 – Tom Davies (1712-1785), actor and bookseller. It was at his bookshop in Russell Street, Covent Garden, that Johnson and Boswell first met.
12 – The Thrales and Johnson visited France in 1775 (see *The French Journals of Mrs Thrale & Dr Johnson*, ed. by Tyson & Guppy, 1932).
15 – James McPherson (1736-1796) claimed to have discovered manuscript poems of Ossian, a legendary third-century Irish bard, which he published in 1765. A famous literary controversy ensued, Johnson always claiming, rightly, that the poems were a forgery by McPherson.
15 – Sir Lucas Pepys, MD (1742-1830), President of the Royal College of Physicians. One of the Thrales' doctors and a regular guest at their table.
15 – Henry St John, 1st Viscount Bolingbroke (1678-1751). His *Works* were published after his death by the Scotsman, David Mallet, in 1754 and were attacked by Johnson for 'impiety', though when taxed he admitted that he had not read the work – *Boswell's Life of Johnson*, ed. by Hill & Powell, 1934-50.
18 – Johnson and Mrs Thrale met Lady Cotton and Lady Catherine Wynne during their tour of Wales in 1774. Mrs Thrale described Lady Wynne as 'an empty woman of quality, insolent, ignorant and ill-bred, without either beauty or fortune to atone her faults' – Mrs Thrale's Welsh journal, in *Dr Johnson and Mrs Thrale* by A. M. Broadley, 1910.
18 – Peter King (1736-1783) was 6th Baron of Ockham.
18 – Lady Macdonald lived in Skye and was visited by Johnson and Boswell during their tour of the Hebrides in 1773.
18 – Thomas Lawrence (1711-1783), physician and medical writer. One of Mr Thrale's doctors.
19 – It is possible that the Harriet Poole referred to is the so-called 'Lady of Lavant', who was a friend of Blake's patron, William Hayley.
19 – Ralph Plumbe was Mr Thrale's nephew.
20 – The Mrs Langton referred to was the mother of Bennet Langton (1737-1801). A famous Greek scholar, he was one of Johnson's closest friends. 'The earth does not bear a worthier man than Bennet Langton,' he once said – *Boswell's Life*.
20 – Richard Cumberland (1732-1811) was a playwright and novelist.

20 – George Romney (1734-1802), painter.
25 – Johnson was very fond of amateur scientific experiments which he often conducted with Mrs Thrale's help.
25 – Brighthelmstone = Brighton.
26 – Francis Barber (1745 ?-1801), Johnson's negro servant. He came to Johnson when he was seven and remained with him until his (Johnson's) death.
27 – Dr Charles Burney (1726-1814), musician. Father of Fanny and close friend of the Thrales. 'Dr Burney is a man for all the world to love' – Johnson, in *Diary and Letters of Madame D'Arblay* (Fanny Burney), ed. by her niece, 1842-46.
27 – Christopher Smart (1722-1771), poet who went mad and died in the debtors prison.
28 – David Garrick (1717-1779) was one of Johnson's oldest friends. They both came from Lichfield and Garrick was a pupil of Johnson's when for a short time he ran a school at Edial in Staffordshire. According to Johnson, when they came up to London together in 1737, Johnson had 2½d in his pocket and Garrick 1½d. Johnson wrote Garrick's famous epitaph, '... that stroke of death which has eclipsed the gaiety of nations and impoverished the public stock of harmless pleasure'.
33 – Lord Tavistock, son of the Duke of Bedford, died in 1767 after a hunting accident.
36 – Thomas Barnard (1728-1806) was Dean of Derry.
   My first shuts out thieves from your house or your room
   My second expresses a Syrian Perfume
   My whole is The Man in whose converse was shar'd
   The strength of the Bar and the sweetness of Nard
                              – Johnson, in *Boswell's Life*.
37 – Mrs Thrale's mother, Mrs Salusbury, fell out with Johnson when, tired of her perpetual concern with foreign affairs, he began to write in the newspapers about imaginary battles between the Russians and the Turks. When Mrs Salusbury discovered the deception she was furious and they were not reconciled for several years.
38 – Abandon all hope, you who enter!
38n – I would write a novel like everyone else, but life is hardly a novel.
39 – Miss Hill Boothby, who died in 1756, was a close family friend of Johnson's.
40 – The blind woman was Miss Anna Williams (1706-1783), who lived with Johnson from 1752 till her death. She wrote poems as well as acting as his housekeeper after the death of his wife.

[131]

40 – The Scotch wench was Poll Carmichael. Johnson said of her: 'Poll is a stupid slut; I had some hopes of her at first; but when I talked to her tightly and closely, I could make nothing of her; she was wiggle-waggle, and I could never persuade her to be categorical' – Fanny Burney's *Diary*.

40 – The woman whose father once lived at Lichfield was Mrs Desmoulins who joined Johnson's household when his wife was still alive. (See the fascinating conversation between her and Boswell in *Boswell: The Applause of the Jury*, ed. by Lustig & Pottel, 1981.)

40 – The superannuated surgeon was Robert Levett (1705-1782), who practised among the poor of London.

45 – 'The Club' was founded in 1764. The original ten members met at the Turk's Head in Gerrard Street, Soho. The Club was enlarged to twenty in 1773 and to twenty-six in 1777.

46 – Abbé du Resnel, author of *Analyse de l'histoire philosophique des établissemens et du commerce des Européens dans les deux Indes*, 1770.

50 – Soame Jenyns (1704-1787), MP for Cambridge and Commissioner for the Board of Trade. He wrote a poem on dancing and *A Free Enquiry into the Nature and Origin of Evil*, 1757, which Johnson savagely attacked in the *Literary Magazine*.

53 – *The False Alarm*, 1770, was written in defence of the Government for refusing John Wilkes admission to the House of Commons although he had been elected Member for Middlesex. 'It was wonderful to see how a prejudice in favour of a government in general, and an aversion to popular clamour, could blind and contract such an understanding as Johnson's in this particular case' – *Boswell's Life*.

53 – Burke's speech was *On Conciliation with America*, delivered on March 22nd, 1775.

55 – In 1742 Johnson was employed by Thomas Osborne, a bookseller, to make a catalogue of the Earl of Oxford's books. 'Sir, he was impertinent to me and I beat him' – Johnson, in *Boswell's Life*.

56 – Mrs Brooke was the wife of the chaplain to the English garrison in Quebec, Rev. John Brooke.

56 – Mr William Rose was a Chiswick schoolmaster.

56 – Johnson is presumably incorrect when he says Matthew Buckinger wrote with his toes: a German, he was born without arms or legs.

61 – The Misses Pitcheses were the daughters of Sir Abraham Pitches, a neighbour of the Thrales at Streatham.

62 – The poor man, who had not noticed, went on fighting – and he was dead.

65 – Robert Vansittart (1728-1789) was professor of Civil Law at Oxford.

65 – 'Johnson was observing the other day . . .' This is one of many excellent passages which Mrs Thrale did not include in her published *Anecdotes*.

66 – 'I who knew perfectly well what this was . . .' A reference to Johnson confiding to Mrs Thrale his fears of insanity. (See notes pp. 111, 115*n* below.)

66 – The eagle does not catch flies.

66 – Charles Churchill (1731-1764), poet. Described by Johnson as 'a shallow fellow', he retaliated by satirising him in his poem 'The Ghost', 1762.

67 – The true Christian always finds that his task is beyond him.

75 – If he who conquers lions,
  By a fair lady is ravaged;
  Let him either be shamed for being puny
  Or her for being so savage.

78 – Admiral George Anson (1697-1762), Admiral of the Fleet. Later Lord Anson of Sorberton.

78 – I applaud this act of gratitude: as he owes everything to the winds, it is right that he should build the winds a temple. (For this, and other translations from the Latin, I am grateful to Jasper Griffin.)

79 – Three poets in three distant ages born
  Greece, Italy, and England did adorn.
  The first in loftiness of thought surpassed;
  The next in Majesty; in both the last.
  The force of nature could no further go;
  To make a third she joined the former two.
     – Dryden

79 – Sir Joseph Banks (1743-1820), naturalist, and President of the Royal Society. He accompanied Captain Cook on his voyage to Australia in 1768.

79 – This goat's milk never failed in two circuits of the globe. This is her reward: she is second only to the goat which suckled the infant Jupiter.

81 – Charlotte Brent and Guadagni were popular singers of the period.

82 – I wander over a country where the bare crags lift their shapeless rocks to the clouds, where the harsh soil mocks the vain toil of the husbandman. I roam among a people whose savage life is adorned by no refinement; primitive and uncouth, it is grimy with the smoke of

the cottage. Amid the roughness of my long wandering, amid the harsh sounds of an unknown tongue, I wonder constantly how fares my dear *Thralia*. Whether as a loyal wife she is soothing the cares of her husband, or as a kind mother tending her children, or as an industrious reader nourishing her mind with new books: may she reward my devotion by remembering me with devotion, and may she deserve to have me make the shores of Skye re-echo the dear name of *Thralia*.

82 – William Warburton (1698-1779), Bishop of Gloucester, Shakespearean commentator and scholar.

82 – Col. George Bodens, an officer in the Coldstream Guards and an old friend of Mr Thrale. He was very fat, suffered from a stammer and was once the victim of a cruel hoax when, in 1762, the *Gentleman's Magazine* announced the death of 'Colonel Bodens, a remarkably large man'.

82 – Samuel Foote (1720-1777), born in Truro, was a famous comic actor, satirist and playwright. He was buried in Westminster Abbey.

84 – Nearby is buried Hester Mary, daughter of Sir Thomas Cotton, Baronet, of Combermere, Chester, and wife of John Salusbury, Gentleman, of Flint. Gifted with beauty and character, loved by all, devoted to her family; in languages and arts so educated that in company her conversation was charming, her views refined, her good sense admirable, her wit delightful; so skilful in keeping the balance that amid her household business she delighted in literature, and amid the joys of literature she was a scrupulous housewife. Wished a long life by many, she fell sick of an incurable cancer; and she left the earth in the hope of a better life. Born 1706, Married 1739, Died 1773.

85 – 'To robbers furious'. This was the only verse of Dr Johnson's that Mrs Thrale never published.

85 – Dr Arthur Collier (1707-1777), a lawyer who taught the young Mrs Thrale Latin, Criticism and Logic.

86 – Elizabeth Montague (1722-1800), the famous literary hostess, known as 'Queen of the Blues'.

86 – Thomas Chubb (1679-1747), a deistical writer and former glovemaker from Salisbury, described by Alexander Pope in a letter to John Gay, 1730, as 'a wonderful phenomenon of Wiltshire' – *Letters of Alexander Pope*, selected by Butt, 1960. The reference is to Johnson's *Dictionary of the English Language*, 1755, in which he included quotations under many of the words to illustrate their usage.

86 – James Harris (1709-1780), a philosopher and grammarian. 'There is a famous joke of Charles Townsend's concerning him – when he was

introduced into the House of Commons – who is this Harris says the witty Charles – why *James* Harris replies somebody – the great Logician who has written one book about Grammar and one about Virtue; and who brings him here then enquires Townsend – he will find neither Grammar nor Virtue in this house' – Mrs Thrale, in *Thraliana, the Diary of Mrs Hester Lynch Thrale (Later Mrs Piozzi) 1776-1809*, ed. by Balderston, 1942.

86 – Rose Fuller (d. 1777) was MP for Rye.

86 – The odd book was Maurice Morgann's *Essay on the Dramatic Character of Sir John Falstaff*, 1777. It was Morgann who once asked Johnson whether he thought Derrick or Smart was the better poet, to which the Doctor gave his famous reply, 'Sir, there is no settling the point of precedency between a louse and a flea' – *Boswell's Life*.

87 – Mrs Jackson was the wife of a chemist, one of two brothers who nearly ruined Mr Thrale's brewing business with a scheme to brew beer using neither malt nor hops.

89 – 'The phrase *Et in Arcadia Ego* is first found in a picture by Guercino (1590-1666)' – *Oxford Companion to English Literature*, ed. by Harvey, 1932.

89 – William Fitzherbert of Derby (d. 1772), a friend of Johnson's.

92 – Rev. George Graham (d. 1767) was assistant master at Eton and author of a masque *Telemachus*, which was never performed.

92 – Oliver Goldsmith (1728-1774), Irish playwright and poet, a close friend of Johnson and the Thrales. The play that was hissed was *The Good-Natured Man*, 1768.

94 – Perhaps our name too will be mingled with theirs.

94 – Perhaps our name will be mingled with *theirs*!

94 – He hides the deep pain in his heart.

95 – Marplot was a character in *The Busybody*, a comedy by Susannah Centlivre (1667?-1723).

96 – 'I was one day examining a lad . . .' This was Ralph Plumbe. (See note p. 19 above.)

98 – Sir Robert Walpole (1676-1745), Prime Minister.

98 – Hawkins Browne (1705-1760), parodist. 'Isaac Hawkins Browne, one of the first wits of this country, got into Parliament and never opened his mouth' – Johnson, in *Boswell's Life*.

99 – Spranger Barry (1719-1777), an Irish actor who appeared in Johnson's play *Irene*, 1749.

100 – William Seward, FRS (1747-1799), editor of *Anecdotes of Some Distinguished Persons*, 1795, and 'a great favourite at Streatham' – Johnson, in *Boswell's Life*.

100 – Thomas Cumming (d. 1774), known as 'the fighting Quaker'. In 1758 he was put in charge of an expedition to capture Senegal which he claimed could be done without any fighting. He suffered greatly when he found this to be impossible and his troops were forced to resort to bloodshed. An anonymous letter attacking him was printed in some papers.
101 – Francis Fawkes (1721-1777), poet and divine. He made several translations of Classical poets.
107 – My Master = Mr Thrale.
108 – My Mistress = Mrs Thrale. A gallina is a guinea fowl.
110 – Hugo Grotius (1583-1645), a Dutch statesman and theologian whose *De Veritate Religionis Christianae* greatly impressed Johnson.
111 – Johnson's secret, to which Mrs Thrale makes a number of guarded references, is his fear of insanity, which he confided to her alone. In 1773 he asked her to lock him up in his room and possibly to tie him up and beat him (see note p. 66 above and below). Such treatment at the time was widely used to cure insanity and it would be a mistake for amateur Freudians to read too much into it. (For a full discussion of these passages see *Samuel Johnson* by Walter Jackson Bate, 1978.)
115*n* – 'Fetters & Padlocks' (see note above). From this it appears that Johnson was not only locked up but fettered as well. When Mrs Thrale's effects were auctioned in Manchester in 1823, they included a padlock labelled 'Johnson's padlock'.
115 – Sir John Lade, Bt (1759-1838) was Henry Thrale's nephew.
116 – Daniel Charles Solander (1736-1782) was a Swedish naturalist who accompanied Captain Cook on his first voyage round the world.
117 – George Psalmanazar (1679-1763) was a Frenchman who came to England in 1703 passing himself off as a Formosan. He wrote a fraudulent book, *Historical and Geographical Description of Formosa*, 1704, and invented a Formosan language of his own. He later confessed to his imposture and became pious.
120 – Zachary Pearce (1690-1774) was Bishop of Rochester. The only person, says Boswell, who gave any help to Johnson when he was compiling his dictionary.
121 – Elijah Impey (1732-1809) was Chief Justice of Bengal, 1774-1789.
123 – Fanny Burney (1752-1840), novelist and diarist, was a very close friend of Mrs Thrale's who later fell out with her over Piozzi. Johnson was devoted to her. The book mentioned is *Cecilia*, 1782.
123 – Molly Aston (1706-1765), a Lichfield friend of Johnson's.

123 – Lovely Mary, you have persuaded me to desire freedom; that I may keep my freedom, adieu lovely Mary!

124 – William Windham (1750-1810), Whig statesman. He visited Johnson on his deathbed. Later he became a friend and ally of William Cobbett.

124 – Boswell was also fascinated by the bits of orange peel that Johnson kept in his pocket. Johnson would only admit that he scraped them and let them dry, but refused to go further. '*Boswell*: "Then the world must be left in the dark. It must be said (assuming a mock solemnity) he scraped them, and let them dry, but what he did with them next he never could be prevailed upon to tell." *Johnson*: "Nay sir, you should say it more emphatically:– he could not be prevailed upon, even by his dearest friends, to tell." ' – *Boswell's Life*.

However, in a letter to Miss Boothby in 1755, Johnson recommends ground orange peel, mixed in port, as an effective remedy for 'indigestion and lubricity of the bowels' – *Letters to and from the Late Samuel Johnson, LL.D.*, ed. by Mrs Piozzi, 1788. He probably used it himself for this purpose.